WHERE DID
GOD
COME FROM?

A HANDBOOK OF ANSWERS TO DIFFICULT QUESTIONS

WHERE DID GOD COME FROM?

A HANDBOOK OF ANSWERS TO DIFFICULT QUESTIONS

BY

PHILIP DELRE

Voice Publishing USA

Where Did God Come From?
A Handbook of Answers to Difficult Questions

Philip DelRe

Unless otherwise indicated, Scripture quotations taken from the New American Standard Bible, Copyright @ 1960, 1962, 1963, 1968, 1971, 1972, 1973, 1975, 1977, 1995 by The Lockman Foundation. Used by permission. (www.Lockman.org)

ISBN 978-0-9677520-7-5

Printed in the United States of America.

Please visit our website for other helpful resources:

www.voice-wilderness.org

For information regarding speaking engagements, please contact:
Voice in the Wilderness Ministries at (815) 547-0765.

Contents

What People Are Saying About The Man, The Ministry, And The Materials

"Philip DelRe has excelled in bringing together powerful thoughts on a most important theme."

—Ray Comfort
The Way of the Master TV Series with Kirk Cameron.
Evangelist, Author, & Speaker

"Phil DelRe powerfully communicates the Gospel and overflows with a passion to reach the lost."

—Dr. Robert Coleman
Author of the best selling: *The Master Plan of Evangelism*.
Former Dean of the Billy Graham International School of
Evangelism and currently a professor at Gordon-Conwell.

"Phil DelRe's tract: *God's Three Witnesses* is the finest Gospel tract I have ever seen." His book, *The Fear of Man Vs. The Fear Of God* touched my heart. It really is a clarion call to action."

—Dr. David Larsen
Professor of Preaching Emeritus at Trinity Evangelical Divinity
School and author of 18 books; including the 900 page *History
of Preaching*; published by Kregel.

"In an era of fadism and fashionable substitutes for true scriptural principles, the ministry of Phil DelRe is a ray of hope for the church. Phil has tapped into the mode of true Gospel evangelism that has proved so mighty in the past. For anyone desirous of seeing the type of deep and thorough heart work that so characterized the church in better days, Phil should not only be heard but studied."

—Reddit Andrews
Director of chapel, Trinity International University

"In a fear filled world, Philip DelRe has written a compelling manual to guide us to God's peace, wisdom, security, and the abundant life worth living. He maps it out so strategically that we can die for the cause, and celebrate through all eternity that it was the best of all ways to live. In *The Fear of Man Vs. The Fear Of God*, Phil's message is clear for all of us who want to be well anchored in God and to serve His great redemptive cause. Read it! be strengthened; Be more focused, and ready to make your God-sized mark. This is a must read!"

—Dr. Bob Griffin
President Rockford Renewal Ministries Author: *Firestorms of Revival: How Historic Moves of God Happened and Will Happen Again*, Creation House.

"Phil's message is right from the Father heart of God."

—Ray Sanders
Director of Christian Friends of Israel

"It's a terrific message—and I can understand listening to it why it had such power. You're quite right in saying it's nothing more than the word of God, but you, of course, presented it very effectively and made the case very powerfully."

—Chuck Colson
Chairman/Founder of Prison Fellowship

"That was the clearest and most complete evangelistic message I have ever heard. I doubt that there was a hard heart left in the room. You need to get this published so the whole world can read it."

—Todd Wendorf
Former Associate Pastor at Saddleback Community Church

"I have been attending seminars for over 40 years, and your presentation was the most direct presentation of the Gospel I have heard."

Pastor from *Beyond Amsterdam 2000 Conference*
Sponsored by the Billy Graham Evangelistic Association and the Evangelical Fellowship of Zambia.

"Of all the ministries that come in to this institution, you and Manny Mills have the most fruitful."

Chaplain Bill Gholson
Ret. Vienna Correctional Center

"Without a doubt Philip DelRe is anointed. When Philip came to our church he spoke on The Fear of Man. The response was tremendous. The Holy Spirit dealt deeply with our hearts and the altar call lasted well over thirty minutes—not by manipulation but by genuine conviction. Philip DelRe and Voice in the Wilderness Ministries is unique, relevant and timely."

—Todd Greiner
Senior pastor of *Community of Faith* Church for over 20 years
and founder of *Church Without Walls* in Southern Illinois.

"Phil DelRe is a Ten Commandments scholar."

—Bob Cornuke
International adventurer and explorer. Author of: *In Search of
the Mountain of God. The Discovery of the Real Mt. Sinai.*

"I absolutely love your book, *God the Final Frontier*. I want my whole family to read it. Your facts on the universe and the Trinity were fascinating!"

—Debra Moffett
Co-host of the Harvest Show and former Miss America 1983

"Your message on law and grace was the most fantastic, fantastic, fantastic sermon I've ever heard in my life."

—Tim & Sarah Brown
Students, Trinity International Divinity School

"Last spring I heard you speak in the undergraduate chapel at Moody. After your message I picked up a tape, and I have listened to that tape at least twenty times. That was the first day I ever heard such a clear explanation of the Gospel in such a Biblical way."

—David Lieske
M. Div. Student, Moody Bible Institute

"I just read your booklet on Jehovah's Witnesses. It is the best resource I have found to refute their false doctrine. I have never seen anything worded better. Your argument is indisputable."

—Dominic Digangi
Former national speaker for the Jehovah's Witnesses

"The day you preached on *The Fear of Man* we had 940 requests for copies of that message! You broke the record!"

—Harvest Church

"I invited Phil DelRe to our church to challenge our hearts in personal evangelism. That is exactly what we received. Phil was well received by all groups in our church. Young and old were blessed. His passion and experience translated into a powerful challenge to our souls!"

—Rodney Tolleson
Pastor of Community Bible Church, DeMotte, IN

Chapter One

Where Did God Come From?

Try to imagine nothing exists. There is no sun, no moon, no stars, and no galaxies. There are no elements such as carbon, hydrogen, nitrogen or oxygen. There are no such things as time, space, matter or energy. There is no universe, no God, nothing! Socrates defined it this way,

> "Nothing is what rocks dream about."

Here's the point; if there ever was a time when nothing but nothing existed, then nothing would exist now, therefore something must be eternal! I love how the late Dr. Walter Martin used to say it,

> "If anything now exists, either something is eternal, or no
> one plus nothing, equals everything."

There is one thing that most scientists, theologians, and philosophers agree on, and it's this. You have only two choices: either God is eternal and uncreated, or matter is eternal and uncreated.

Prominent evolutionist George Wald, biochemist and Nobel Laureate from Harvard University said,

> "When it comes to the origin of life, we have only two possibilities as to how life arose. One is spontaneous generation arising to evolution; the other is a supernatural creative act of God. There is no third possibility...Spontaneous generation was scientifically disproved one hundred years ago by Louis Pasteur, Spellanzani, Reddy and others. That leads us scientifically to only one possible conclusion—that life arose as a supernatural creative act of God...I will not accept that philosophically because I do not want to believe in God. Therefore,

I choose to believe in that which I know is scientifically impossible, spontaneous generation arising to evolution." [1]

How Impossible Is It?

"Fred Hoyle and his colleague Chandra Wickramasinghe (*both world famous physicists*), calculated the odds that all the functional proteins necessary for life might originate by chance. They came up with a figure of one chance in 1040,000 (that's a 1 with 40,000 zeros after it)." [2] It is believed that the number of atoms in the known universe is 1080. That is ten with 80 zeros after it! According to the mathematical science of probability, if a number has more than 50 zeros after it, the odds of that happening by chance is virtually impossible. Hoyle has adopted the theory that life must have come from other planets. That is circular reasoning.

Einstein Meets Moses

It was 1910 when Albert Einstein's Theory of Relativity was first published. His mathematical equation provided a basis for proof that the universe and time itself had a beginning. Einstein's formula revealed that time, space, and matter (which is energy) had a beginning. Interestingly, his theory (which has never been dis-proven) fit the biblical model perfectly. The very first verse in the Bible says: "In the beginning God created the heavens and the earth." In the beginning (that's time), God created (that's energy), the heavens (that's space), and the earth (that's matter)!

Science Speaks

Since Einstein's theory (which has been proven accurate to within five decimal points) shows that time, space, and matter had a beginning, then our only other option is staring us in the face: God is eternal and uncreated!

Therefore, as Norman Geisler states it, "Asking the question, where did God come from? is a nonsensical question. It contains the false assumption that God was created or had a beginning and then asks: how is that possible? It's like asking, where did the bachelor get his wife? Or, what does blue sound like? Bachelors by definition do not have wives, and sight is not in the category of sound." [3] In the same sense, God is not in the category of created things. The question itself is fatally flawed. Asking the wrong question does not generally produce the right answer. A better question to begin with is, "Why is there something rather than nothing?" As for the question of cause and effect, that only applies to things that have a beginning.

God Lives In Another Dimension

"Since the universe reveals time, space and matter, God must be outside of time, space and matter. We can thus conclude that God is timeless and eternal. We can also conclude that God is immaterial since He transcends space.

"To have created the universe, in all of its incredible vastness, out of nothing, God must be omnipotent. To have created the universe with such precision and intricate design, perfect for the existence of human life on earth, God must be omniscient.

"To have made an unending series of design choices requires that God be personal, for an inanimate, impersonal thing cannot make choices. God's personality is also evidenced in the fact that He created personal human beings.

"Absolute moral truth is absolute proof of a universal moral lawgiver. All these characteristics are consistent with what the Bible reveals about God."[4]

The Laws Of Logic, Nature, & Morality

In order to have a rational debate with anyone, we must acknowledge that the laws of logic, the laws of nature, and the laws of morality not only exist, but are necessary if we are to communicate in a meaningful way. Let's look at what these laws are and then, (God willing) we will see the insurmountable problems they pose for the unbeliever.

The Law Of Logic

The first law of logic is the law of non-contradiction. This law states that all contradictions are inherently false. You cannot say, "My wife is at home and my wife is not at home." Either both statements are wrong (maybe I'm not married), or one is right and the other is wrong. They cannot both be true at the same time and in the same sense. That is the law of logic. If you think this through carefully, you will realize that only the biblical worldview can account for *why* these laws exist at all.

But, the atheist can say, "I believe the law of logic and I don't believe in God or the Bible!" That may be true; however, in an evolutionary universe the unbeliever cannot provide a reason why logic, natural law, or morality would exist at all!

> "From the standpoint of reality, we understand that God is the basis of all logic. As the ultimate reality, all truth is ultimately found in him. He has created the reality that we know and in which we have discovered the laws of logic. Even Jesus said, 'I am . . . the truth' (John 14:6). He has structured the world in such a way that these laws cannot be denied; however, we did not know God first and then learn logic from Him. He exists as the basis of all logic (in reality), but we discovered logic first and came to know God through it. This is true even if we came to know God through His revelation, because we understood the revelation through logic." [5]

Is the law of non-contradiction in the Bible? Here's an example from 1 John 2:21:

> "I have not written to you because you do not know the truth, but because you do know it, and because no lie is of the truth."

According to the Bible, something is either true or false; it cannot be both true and false at the same time. If the evolutionist wants to live in a world where there are objective standards of truth and right from wrong, and where good and evil are meaningful, he must borrow from the biblical worldview for these concepts to be rational. The idea that we should or should not be rational at all depends on the universal laws of logic and morality. To be rational means you are able to give a reasonable answer for *why* something is good or evil. This the evolutionist cannot do.

The Law Of Nature

Scientific analysis would not be not possible without consistency in nature. Time, space, matter, gravity, etc., must be consistent in order for scientific experimentation to be meaningful. Time is based on the consistency of our solar system. The earth revolves at a constant speed making one revolution every 24 hours while simultaneously orbiting the sun at a traveling velocity of 67,000 miles an hour. Planet Earth makes the 584,000,000 mile journey around the sun once every 365.25 days. Its "on time" arrival record is better than any train or airline in the world!

Consider Our Own Milky Way Galaxy

The Milky Way galaxy is 100,000 light years across and 10,000 light years in diameter at the center. To get from one end of the galaxy to the other, you would have to travel at the speed of light (186,282 miles every second) for 100,000 years! The earth is 26,000 light years from the center of the galaxy. If you were to take a commercial airliner from earth to the center of our own Milky Way galaxy, traveling at 550 miles an hour, it would take you 278 quadrillion years to get there!

Not only do all the planets in our solar system revolve around the sun, but the entire Milky Way galaxy (containing 100-200 billion stars) revolves once every 250 million years! From our position in space, we are being hurled around the center of the galaxy at an incredible 550,000 miles an hour. What holds all the stars in place as we fly through time and space, around and around like a giant cosmic Ferris-wheel? How much power is required to move it and where does it come from? Why don't the stars collide? Who steers it? How could this happen all by itself? What about the hundreds of billions of other galaxies doing the same thing? Who is directing all this traffic?

Because of the regularity of the physical laws that govern our universe, astronomers can chart the position of planets, moons, stars, and asteroids far into the future with accuracy and precision.

Here is what Albert Einstein said about natural law in his book *The World As I See It*:

> "The harmony of natural law reveals an intelligence of such superiority that, compared with it, all the systematic thinking of human beings is an utterly insignificant reflection.

> ". . . it seems to me, (this) is the attitude of even the most intelligent human being toward God. We see a universe marvelously arranged and obeying certain laws, but only dimly

understand these laws. Our limited minds cannot grasp the mysterious force that moves the constellations." [6]

The Moral Law

The bricklayer uses a plumb line, a level, and a square. He has a perfect point of reference. It takes a straight line to see where and how much a crooked line is off the mark. If you were out to sea in a dense fog, unable to see the stars and without a compass, you would have no way to determine north from south. In the same sense, without the God of the Bible, there is no reference point for anything!

Why Do We Have To Use The God Of The Bible?

We have to use the God of the Bible because you will not find a perfect moral standard in any other so-called holy book! The Ten Commandments are exclusive to the Bible. Just as mathematics is a perfect science, so is God's moral law. Psalm 19:7 says,

"The law of the LORD is perfect converting the soul."

How do we know this is *God's* law? First of all, God's moral law is universal. Every man from the beginning of time until the end of the world, whether or not he has ever even heard of Jesus or even seen a Bible, *knows* in his *heart* it's *wrong* to murder, it's *wrong* to steal, it's *wrong* to lie, it's *wrong* to have another man's wife, etc. He *knows it instinctively*, just as sure as the birds fly south for the winter. The Bible says God's law is written on every man's heart (Romans 2:15).

Secondly, if everyone obeyed God's moral law (the Ten Commandments), we would live in a perfect world! The Ten Commandments can be distilled down to two; stated positively they are: love God with all your heart and love your neighbor as yourself. Now think this through.

The Incredible Power Of The Moral Law

When God says, "Thou shalt not lie", He is by implication saying, "Thou shall tell the truth." I challenge you right now to take a minute and try to imagine what would happen to our world if everyone stopped lying tomorrow. What would happen to our political and criminal justice systems if everyone always told the truth? What about the civil courts? How would this policy affect our financial institutions, and the retail sales industry? What would happen to the world economy? What political impact would this have on the nations, and on relationships between husbands and wives, parents and children, employers and employees? And that's just *one* commandment!

Walk through each one of the Ten Commandments and ask yourself the same question, "What would happen if everyone in the world began to obey this commandment?" Try it with number 8, "Thou shalt not steal." The number one crime in America is retail theft. What would happen to our world if no one *ever* took what did not belong to them again? How would it affect the economy, our peace of mind, and the prices of goods and services? None of us would ever have to lock our doors. If everyone obeyed the Ten Commandments, there would be no more war, no more prisons, we would no longer need armies, and the police would only be needed to direct traffic! The whole idea is incredible. There is no other religion, philosophy, or system of thought that would so radically change our world for the better like obedience to the Ten Commandments.

If everyone loved God and loved their neighbors according to this standard we would live in a perfect world! That is one of the reasons we know the Ten Commandments are divinely inspired. This same idea is expressed in the New Testament in Romans 13:8-10,

> Owe no one anything except to love one another, for he who loves his neighbor has fulfilled the law. For the commandments, "You shall not commit adultery," "You shall not murder," "You shall not steal," "You shall not bear false witness," "You shall not covet," and if there is any other commandment, are all summed up in this saying, namely, "You shall love your neighbor as yourself." Love does no harm to a neighbor; therefore love is the fulfillment of the law.

What Does A Lawless World Look Like?

In the evolutionary worldview, it's a dog-eat-dog world—literally! It's perfectly normal for lions to eat other animals. You wouldn't put a lion in jail for that, would you? Of course not; it's the law of the jungle, the survival of the fittest. In this evolutionary model, Jeffery Dahmer, the homosexual cannibal from Wisconsin, was just doing what comes naturally. You wouldn't put a man in jail for that, would you? This is what he said in an interview on NBC television:

"If a person doesn't think there is a God to be accountable to, then what's the point of trying to modify your behavior to keep it within acceptable range? That's how I thought, anyway. I always believed the theory of evolution is truth that we all just came from slime. When we died, you know, that was it; there's nothing."

Dateline: Berlin, Germany, 1936

Adolph Hitler was also a Darwinian evolutionist. In his worldview, natural selection meant the survival of the fittest. According to 'der Führer', the final solution to the world's problems was *not* to love your neighbor, but to kill off the weaker races. In his mind, they were nothing more than "useless eaters". Hitler, believing the Aryan race to be superior, was attempting to expedite the evolutionary process!

Two of the weakest races, according to Hitler, were Jews and Africans. How Hitler arrived at those conclusions is a mystery. The Jews have produced many of the greatest minds in science and the Africans have produced many of the greatest athletes in the world. How ironic that in 1936, when the world was on the verge of World War II, that the Olympics were held in Berlin, Germany. Adolph Hitler watched helplessly (then walked out) as Jesse Owens, an African American, won four gold medals, breaking three world records in the process. His long-jump record held for 26 years! Ironically, when WWII ended, it was the God-fearing Americans and their allies who set the Jews free from the concentration camps, while Hitler committed suicide.

In all of recorded history, there is not a single example of a nation or a corporation that declined morally that did not eventually pass into poverty and then oblivion. The United States is a perfect example of how God exalts a nation that builds its foundation on Biblical principles. We also see what happens when that nation turns away from God. No nation, corporation, church, or family can endure long-term without moral leadership and virtue as a priority in the hearts of its people.

The Laws Of Logic, Mathematics, Nature, And Morality Were Not Invented, They Were Discovered!

Here are some of the biblical passages that explain why:

- Genesis 1:1—"In the beginning God created the heavens and the earth."

- Genesis 8:22—"While the earth remains, seedtime and harvest, and cold and heat, and summer and winter, and day and night shall not cease."

- John 1:3—"All things came into being by Him, and apart from Him nothing came into being that has come into being."

According to Colossians 1:15, "He (Jesus Christ) holds all things together", and in Hebrews 13:8 we read, "Jesus Christ is the same yesterday, today, and forever." This accounts for the consistency we observe in the universe!

Is It Right To Teach Children The Bible?

The evolutionist often says, "You should not try to force your ideas on us." But aren't they trying to force their ideas on us by saying that? The Christian has a reason for believing in an absolute moral standard that applies to everyone. It is wrong to lie because there is a God in heaven who says it's wrong. He created all of us and He knows what is best. The Bible contains the greatest moral code known to man.

Evolutionists might say, "What is best for the majority is what is right!" Adolph Hitler convinced most of Germany that what he was doing was right and he was dead wrong!

As for those in the scientific community who still hold on to the rotting corpse of Darwinian Evolution, and are still searching for the missing link, they may want to consider the words of one of the world's leading rocket scientists. Robert Jastrow is an astrophysicist and the former Director of the National Aeronautics and Space Administration's Goddard Institute. In his book *God and the Astronomers*, he writes,

> "At this moment it seems as though science will never be able to raise the curtain on the mystery of creation. For the scientist who has lived by his faith in the power of reason, the

story ends like a bad dream. He has scaled the mountains of ignorance; he is about to conquer the highest peak; as he pulls himself over the final rock, he is greeted by a band of theologians who have been sitting there for centuries."

Here's The Point

You have two choices. If there is no God, then man is nothing more than an electrochemical blob of accidental living matter that originated from a pool of slime some 15 billion years ago. So as one scumbag to another, since there is no accountability after death, and there is no absolute moral truth in life, let every man do what is right in his own eyes. Give no thought for tomorrow or anybody else. Eat, drink, and be merry, for tomorrow we die.

If that philosophy is either too hard or too soft, this one should be just right. You are a child of God created for a purpose. Love the God who created you with all your heart, mind, soul, and strength. Then love your neighbor as yourself. Do all the good you can, as often as you can, to as many as you can, while you can. It's more blessed to give than to receive. You'll have no regrets in this life and none in the next!

A Closing Illustration

"The Christians Are Here; Call Out The Lions!"

It was a beautiful Thursday night in Chicago just before 7 p.m. I was walking into the "Super Maximum Security" division of the Cook County jail—one of the most notorious county jails in the United States. As a chaplain, I have been preaching there once, twice, and sometimes three times a week for the last 18 years. It's an absolutely incredible place. On 96 acres, it's the largest county jail in America. It's a city within a city. There are 10,000 men and 1,500 women locked up behind hundreds of thousands of tons of cement and steel. As many as 100,000 men and women will be processed through the jail each year. It has an underground tunnel system connecting 10 of the 11 divisions. It has almost 4,000 full-time employees, and its own hospital. When the first division was constructed in 1929, it included a small room with one piece of furniture—the electric chair—they call it the "Ice House." In 1931 Al Capone became one of its most notorious inmates. In 1971, blues legend B.B. King recorded an album there appropriately titled: *B. B. King—Live at Cook County Jail.* And in 1996, the *Back to God Hour* produced a television special there entitled: *Back to the Streets.* 1 It featured *our* ministry.

"Super Maximum Security" is where they keep the highest-bond and no-bond inmates. Here you will find the most violent men charged with the most heinous crimes. Division 11 is also the newest addition to the jail. At a construction cost of more than $100 million, it's huge, it's all white, and I call it the Taj Mahal. Each block is air conditioned, and furnished with a colored TV. Every inmate gets "three hots and a cot," and the best police protection money can buy. Ironically, they also get a piece of cake or a cookie on their dinner trays!

Once inside, I take the elevator up to the third floor to the security office in order to sign in and pick up my I.D. badge. Security officers will then arrange to have the men escorted to the chapel. On special occasions, we have had as many as 1,200 inmates in the gymnasium for chapel! Exiting the elevator and approaching the security office, I spy an officer sitting at his desk; I have not seen for some time. That's because they are transferred from division to division every year or so just to "shake things up." I have known this particular officer for the last 18 years, and every time I run into him (he's like a Mack Truck) he's taken every opportunity to insult me personally, to mock Christianity, and to openly mock God! I have met some characters over the years, as you might imagine, but this man is in a class by himself.

As I was approaching the security office, he saw me and I saw him. As I walked in, he stood up and assumed the stance of a weight lifter about to try out for the world's record. You know, leaning slightly forward, arms hanging down slightly curled in, flexing his muscles; sort of like a turkey spreading its wings to show off. In a loud voice, with his eyes fixed on me, he barked at the two officers across the room:

"The Christians are here; call out the lions!"

Without hesitation, but rather sheepishly at first, I replied, "Sergeant, I'd like to remind you that it was 2,000 years ago that the Roman Empire was feeding Christians to the lions, and we have the incredible perspective of being able to look back over 2,000 years of recorded history and what do we see?" Getting louder and bolder I said, "There are more

Christians alive at this moment than the total number of people that made up the Roman Empire over its entire 500-year history,

AND THE LIONS AND TIGERS ARE ON THE ENDANGERED-SPECIES LIST. WE'RE NOT AFRAID OF LIONS; BRING 'EM ON!"

I looked at him, and his jaw dropped. I looked at the two officers in the corner, and their mouths were open so wide they could have eaten a banana sideways! The sergeant, only slightly discombobulated, broke the silence and ordered the officers to, "Call chapel"!

So, what is the point of this story? Simply this: when you're right about God, and you're right with God, you never have to be intimidated by the world, the flesh, or the devil himself. And it's okay to get excited about Jesus! As an interesting follow-up to this story, that officer is now my best friend at the jail. He actually goes out of his way to help us bring more men to chapel. Best of all, he is now asking me questions about the Bible!

A Final Thought

The most normal, natural, sane, rational intelligent thing you can do is to love the God Who created you and become a disciple of Jesus Christ. Knowing God is the key that unlocks all the treasures of wisdom and knowledge man needs to live successfully. The greatest questions are all answered by having a personal relationship with God through the Lord Jesus Christ. When you know who you are in relation to who He is, you know:

1. Who you are. 2. Where you came from. 3. Why you are here. 4. Where you are going. 5. You have someone to love and be loved by. 6. You have something to do. 7. You have something to hope for.

The first verse in the Bible may be the most controversial of the more than 31, 000 verses found within its pages. If Genesis 1: 1 is not true, then there is no such thing as absolute moral truth, because in an evolutionary universe there is no basis for it. And since we know that is false (for to deny absolutes is logically self-defeating), then the account given in Genesis 1:1 is consistent with the existence of absolute truth (whereas evolution is not).

If evolution is true then life has no meaning, and the world is an inexplicable riddle. If the Bible *is* correct, then the origin of the human race is satisfactorily explained-love has value and life has meaning.

End Notes

1. George Wald: *Scientific American*, August, 1954.

2. Fred Heeren: *Show Me God* (Wheeling. Searchlight Publications, 1995) p. 183.

3. Norm Geisler: *I Don't Have Enough Faith to be an Atheist.* (Wheaton. Crossway Books, 2004).

4. Adapted from Ron Rhodes: *Answering the Objections of Atheists.* (Harvest House Publishers), 2006, p. 56.

5. Norman Geisler and Ronald Brooks: *Come Let Us Reason—An Introduction to Logical Thinking.* (Baker), p.17.

6. Denis Brian, *Einstein: A Life* (New York: John Wiley and Sons, 1996), p. 186.

To learn more about the power of the Ten Commandments in evangelism see the author's book, *Jesus Christ the Master Evangelist—How to Present the Gospel the Way Jesus Did*. www.voice-wilderness.org

Small Group Questions

1. What are the four things that Einstein's Theory of Relativity revealed that are also found in Genesis 1:1?

2. What did Einstein's theory tell us about the universe?

3. There are only two possibilities: either _____ is eternal and uncreated or, _____ is eternal and uncreated.

4. How do we know that something must be eternal?

5. In order to have a rational discussion with someone, one must accept three laws that are self-evident truths. What are they?

6. Give a brief explanation of each of the three laws.

7. Why must atheists borrow from the Bible to use logic?

8. What are the moral distinctions between the God of the Bible and other religions?

9. How do we know the Ten Commandments are divinely inspired?

10. How does immorality destroy nations, corporations, churches and families?

Chapter Two

Why Should I Believe the Bible?

The Bible is utterly and absolutely unique among *all* other books for several reasons. It not only refers to itself as "The Word of God", but offers many infallible proofs that it is. The "Word" refers to the Living Word—Jesus Christ—and the written Word—the Bible. Upon close examination, the serious student will discover that the Word of God stands alone. There is no possible term of comparison between the Bible and Jesus Christ and any other so-called "holy book" or religious leader in history. Keep reading and you'll see why.

God made sure no one could ever claim the Bible was a man-made conspiracy. It was written over the course of 1,500 years, on three continents—Europe, Asia, and Africa. It was written in three languages—Hebrew, Aramaic, and Greek. It was produced by 40 different writers, and yet it has a beginning, middle, and an end. Its main theme is the redemption of man and its main character is Jesus Christ. It speaks on hundreds of controversial topics in perfect harmony. Completed 1,900 years ago, the Bible tells us how the world began and how it will end; it reveals the purpose of man, and the future of mankind.

Prophecy

Bible prophecy is empirical proof that the Scriptures are divinely inspired. The reason is obvious. No human being can even come close to predicting the future with 100 percent accuracy. Only a person with omniscience can do that.

Dr. Wilbur Smith, who assembled a personal library of 29,000 volumes, concludes that:

"Whatever one may think of the authority of and the message presented in the book we call the Bible, there is world-wide agreement that in more ways than one it is the most remarkable volume that has ever been produced in these some 5,000 years of writing on the part of the human race.

"It is the only volume ever produced by man, or a group of men, in which is to be found a large body of prophecies relating to individual nations, to Israel, to all the peoples of the earth, to certain cities, and to the coming of one who was to be the Messiah. The ancient world had many different devices for determining the future, known as divination, but not in the entire gamut of Greek and Latin literature, even though they use the words prophet and prophecy, can we find any real specific prophecy of a great historic event to come in the distant future, nor any prophecy of a Savior to arise in the human race." [1]

The Scriptures also contain metaphysical information that transcends the human intellect. From astronomy, to physics, to biology, to prophecy and more, the unbiased student will be forced to the inescapable conclusion that the Bible is a direct revelation from a vastly superior intelligence. The following are just a few examples of God's omniscience.

Physics

As we mentioned in the first chapter, the very first verse in the Bible perfectly parallels one of the greatest and most advanced physics equations ever discovered. Keep in mind that the Scriptures were written thousands of years before scientific research even began. Einstein's Theory of Relativity provided a basis for proof that time, space and matter (which is energy) were not only the foundational facts of science, but each had a beginning (as opposed to being eternal). The implications of this mathematical equation (math being a perfect science) were enormous; it left Einstein (and all the rest of us) staring in the face of God.

Incredibly, the Bible begins with these words, "In the beginning (that's time) God created (that's energy) the heavens (that's space) and the earth (that's matter). And that's just the first verse! Just 5 chapters later we come to . . .

Noah's Ark

In Genesis chapter 6 we have the record of God telling Noah to build the ark. As for the pseudo scientists who mock those who take this story literally, there are a couple of "minor details" they'll need to explain *before* we decide who has the last laugh (there is nothing funny about a lost person, it's only a phrase to make a point).

The author of the book of Genesis gave Noah the exact specifications necessary to build the ark, and to build it right. Here is what is recorded in Genesis 6:14-16:

> "Make yourself an ark of gopherwood; make rooms in the ark, and cover it inside and outside with pitch. And this is how you shall make it: The length of the ark shall be three hundred cubits, its width fifty cubits, and its height thirty cubits. You shall make a window for the ark, and you shall finish it to a cubit from above; and set the door of the ark in its side. You shall make it with lower, second, and third decks."

A cubit is the length of a man's arm from his elbow to the tip of his middle finger (about a foot and a half). Based on the Biblical account, we know (within a matter of inches) how long, how wide and how high Noah's ark was! That means we can test it. Interestingly, it was not until the 20th century that scientists built a scaled down model of Noah's ark using the exact ratios of height, width, and length found in the Genesis account. They wanted to test the sea worthiness of its design. Estimating the weight for the proper ballast, they put their experiment to the test in a large tank filled with water. Then they produced waves, gradually increasing their intensity.

What they discovered was astounding. It wouldn't sink! They concluded that a ship built to those specifications would have been one of the most sea worthy vessels ever constructed. What are the odds of Noah guessing how to build a ship of this magnitude and getting it right? About the same odds you would have of being struck by lightning twice in the same spot. How did Noah know this? He didn't. God did.

Here is another inexplicable fact (humanly speaking) about Noah's flood. Scientists have discovered marine fossils on mountain peaks all over the world, including Mt. Everest, the highest point on earth. How did the fossils of sea creatures ascend 29,000 feet above sea level? Do our atheistic "scientists" have an explanation for this? Were they flying fish? Or, maybe they came from another planet! The Bible provides the answer in Genesis 7:17-20:

> "Now the flood was on the earth forty days. The waters increased and lifted up the ark, and it rose high above the earth. The waters prevailed and greatly increased on the earth, and the ark moved about on the surface of the waters. And the waters prevailed exceedingly on the earth and all the high hills under the whole heaven were covered. The waters prevailed fifteen cubits upward, and the mountains were covered."

Go to *Answers in Genesis* on the World Wide Web, to learn everything you ever wanted to know about Noah's flood.

History

Another unique thing about the Bible is the fact that God's plan of redemption (the whole point of the Book) is interwoven in and through actual historical events. The Bible's historical accuracy has been verified not only by secular historians, but by more than 100 years of painstaking research by archeologists. Most of the great Bible stories (names, dates, times, places and events) have been discovered by this scientific method and proven to be accurate time and again.

The Bible does not start out, "Once upon a time." The origin of man begins in a real geographical location called the Garden of Eden. Its exact location is revealed in Genesis chapter 2 where we read,

> "Now a river flowed out of Eden to water the garden; and from there it divided and became four rivers."

In Genesis 2:11-14, the Word of God identifies the names and the location of these rivers!

> "The name of the first is Pishon ... the name of the second river is Gihon; it flows around the whole land of Cush. And the name of the third river is Tigris; it flows east of Assyria. And the fourth river is the Euphrates."

Here we are today, approximately 6,000 years later and two of those rivers still exist. The Tigris and the Euphrates rivers meet in a place called "Al Qurnah", which is located in southeastern Iraq.

The Exclusive On Ancient History

Herodotus, the Greek historian, is known as the "father of history" and was a contemporary of Malachi, the writer of the last Old Testament book. But the Bible records events going as far back as Abraham (2,000 years before Christ), and for that matter, it takes us all the way back to the creation of the world! There is *no other book* that can make such a claim.

Reading the Bible, we learn of the Mesopotamian world through the lives of the patriarchs. We see God's plan of redemption played out in the epic drama of the Hebrew people being delivered from slavery in Egypt. What follows is the fascinating account of the children of God marching through the Red Sea, the revelation of God giving the Ten Commandments on Mt. Sinai and the beginning of the nation of Israel.

We learn the rich history of Israel's rise to power under Kings Saul, David and Solomon. We also learn of Israel's downfall because of her sin. The Bible does not cover up the dark side of its greatest characters. The Word of God tells it like it is. Three of its greatest heroes, Moses, King David and the Apostle Paul were all murderers.

Through the life of Daniel we read the history of the Babylonian Empire and King Nebuchadnezzar. Daniel was born during the reign of King Josiah of Judah, who was followed by his son Jehoiakim, who was conquered by Nebuchadnezzar. Daniel's prophecies concerning the future kingdoms that would rule the world were so precise, secular historians and skeptics insist they had to be written after the fact.

Through the eyes of Queen Esther we learn of the Persian Empire under King Ahasuerus and how God used Esther to save her people from annihilation.

It is no coincidence that the hero of the story (Jesus Christ) does not appear until the Roman Empire came to power. The phrase, "All roads lead to Rome" was coined because Rome built roads that made travel much easier. Thus, another phrase was coined. With travel being vastly improved, so were communications. As a result, the Disciples of Christ were credited with "turning the world upside down" with the Gospel!

The New Testament begins in Bethlehem of Judea, in the time of King Herod. Hundreds of names, dates, times, places and events are recorded, leaving an obvious trail for us to follow.

Why did God choose to write the Bible this way? God has revealed Himself and His plan of redemption through history (the past) and through prophecy (the future) so that the nations may *know* that He is the Lord. In Isaiah 46:9-10 God says,

> "Remember the former things long past, for I am God, and there is no other; {I am} God, and there is no one like me, Declaring the end from the beginning and from ancient times things which have not been done, saying, 'My purpose will be established, and I will accomplish all my good pleasure.'"

Astromony

The ancient Egyptians believed that the earth was suspended on five pillars.

The Greeks believed Atlas held the earth on his shoulders.

The Hindus taught that the earth was held up by an elephant, the elephant was on a tortoise, the tortoise was on a serpent, and the serpent was swimming in a cosmic sea. And, it was just a few hundred years ago that most people thought the earth was flat! In fact, *The Flat Earth Society still does!*

In Sura 18:86, *The Koran* says, "the sun sets in a puddle of mud!"

Yet in chapter 26 of Job, the Bible says, "God hangs the earth upon nothing." And in 750 B.C., the 40th chapter of Isaiah told us that "God sits upon the circle of the earth." But, man didn't *know* that until Columbus sailed around the world without falling off!

Before Galileo came along, star gazers believed there were about 2,500 stars. And, just about 2,500 years *before* Galileo, the prophet Jeremiah said, "The host of heaven cannot be numbered" (Jeremiah 33:22). How could Jeremiah possibly have known that? He didn't. God did.

Something Old, Something New
Something Bold, Something True

The Bible is divided into two parts, the Old Testament and the New Testament. This is fascinating. Without the New Testament, the Old

Testament would be incomplete, and without the Old Testament, the New Testament would be utterly incomprehensible! Each is a guide to properly understanding the other. The Old Testament is the foundation upon which the New Testament is built. And the New Testament constantly refers back to the Old Testament to establish its credibility. This is intended to reveal its super-natural origin through prophecy. And just to make doubly sure no one could ever claim the Bible is a man-made conspiracy, there are 400 years of silence between the Old Testament and the New Testament! Through fulfilled prophecy, both testaments point back and forth to the other as positive proof of their divine authenticity and perfect unity. The very first verse in the New Testament forces us to this inescapable conclusion. Matthew 1:1 shows us two things. First, that God always keeps His promises, and secondly, that the Bible is one book!

> "This is the record of the genealogy of Jesus Christ the Son of David, the Son of Abraham."

This verse says in effect, "If you are starting here, you have to go back to Genesis, man!" Who would pick up any other book and start reading right in the middle? Yet, people do that with the Bible, and wonder why they have trouble understanding it. "Starting in Matthew is like walking into a movie half-way through. It's like thinking you are telling a good joke when all you can remember is the punch line."[3]

Without knowing the covenant promises that God made with Abraham and David, Matthew 1:1 would be utterly boring. Yet to those who understand it in the context of the promises made by God in the Old Testament, this verse explodes with excitement! Matthew announces to the world that the promise of a Savior (possibly going back as far as 6,000 years) begins now!

This same principle holds true for more than 1,200 verses in the New Testament. What is the significance of Christ dying on Passover and being raised on First Fruits, were it not for the book of Exodus? What sense would John have made when he said of Jesus, "Behold the Lamb of God who takes away the sin of the world," or, of Jesus when He said, "This is the new covenant in My blood," were it not for the doctrine of the blood atonement in Leviticus?

The sacrificial system of ancient Judaism provided the world with 1,500 years of literal, historical, and theological context, so when Jesus came along and offered Himself as a sacrifice for the sin of the world, this would all make sense.

Numbers Count

Most of us think of Matthew as the first book of the New Testament, and it is. In our modern English translations, Matthew is *also* the 40th book of the 66 that make up the Bible. The number 40 is significant since throughout Scripture, it represents the number of completion.

Furthermore, the Old Testament contains truths that are essential for a proper worldview that are found in *no other source*. For example, only in the book of Genesis do we discover the origin of the universe, of man and his fall into sin, the doctrine of marriage and the family, the establishment of the nations, languages, and the prophetic significance of Israel! Only in the Old Testament are we told of the rebellion in Heaven that turned Lucifer into Satan, and thus the origin of evil, and the promise of a Redeemer.

"The Old Testament worldview is clearly distinct from other worldviews, such as polytheism, pantheism, gnosticism, deism, atheism, and naturalism. The New Testament does not provide another worldview but simply assumes the one taught in the Old Testament."4

I Can Prove The Bible Is True
With One Word— Israel

The Word of God plainly states that the nation of Israel plays a major role in the end-time events of human history, thousands of years in advance. Using Israel as an object lesson, the main theme of the Bible from beginning to end is how God can forgive man's sin without compromising His justice. Simply stated, the Bible is the story of Jesus Christ, the one mediator between God and Man, the Redeemer of all who trust in Him. The story begins and ends in the Holy Land of Israel.

Written thousands of years ago, one recurring theme *throughout* the Bible is the birth, the death, and the rebirth of the nation of Israel. In Ezekiel 36-39 (written 2,500 years ago) God revealed that the Jews would be exiled from Israel (because of her sin), the land would be desolate for a long time, and in the latter days He would bring them back as a nation. History shows that this is precisely what happened!

In A.D. 70, the Roman army destroyed Jerusalem, and the surviving Jews were exiled. Miraculously, they remained a distinct race even though they had no homeland for nearly 1,900 years! After World War II, they began to trickle back into Israel. Then, in May, 1948, they established a second Jewish state, precisely as the Bible predicted!

In Zechariah 14:2, the Bible clearly states that the last war of the world will be fought over Jerusalem (more proof that the Bible is true).

How Miraculous Is Bible Prophecy?

Imagine that I predicted 1,000 years in advance the exact city in which the President of the United States would be born, his exact birth date, his nationality, what family he would come from, what kind of car he would drive, where he would go to school, what his name would be, what his father's and mother's names would be, how old he would be when he died, when and how he would die, plus dozens of his most significant accomplishments—all in specific detail—and I was 100 per cent accurate on every count. Would that be a miracle? That is exactly what the Bible did in reference to Jesus.

According to Ph.D. astrophysicists and other qualified American science professors, the odds of fulfilling the Bible's prophecies *by chance alone* are one out of a number expressed as 1 with 2,000 zeros after it. According to the mathematical science of probability, if a number has more than 50 zeros after it, the odds of that happening by chance is virtually impossible. To put this in perspective, the number of atoms in the known universe is believed to be 1080. That is ten with 80 zeros after it!

The Bible On Life

The main theme of the Bible is God's redeeming love through Jesus Christ. By contrast, the main theme (by actual word-count) of the Koran is the contrast of believers vs. non-believers and former believers. Almost every page extols the virtue of being a Muslim and condemns non-believers as infidels, destined for eternal punishment. If you were to remove every verse exhorting believers and every verse that threatens unbelievers, there would be little left in the Koran.

My point is not to belittle another man's religion but to put the Bible in context. The Bible is the complete and comprehensive book on life. Among its more than 31,000 verses you can find the answer to just about every question you ever wanted to know about life. Some of the topics covered include these: How can I know God, who am I, why am I here, where did I come from, where am I going, is there life after death, do heaven and hell really exist, how do I get there, if God is good why is there evil, what is sin, how can I be forgiven, how can I forgive, how to be a good husband, a good wife, how to have a healthy marriage, how to train children, how to handle money, how to invest money, how to have lasting relationships and on it goes.

There are verses that tell you what to do when you are afraid, anxious, bereaved, defeated, depressed, discouraged, doubting, facing a crisis, when friends fail you, when you are in need of protection, needing guidance, how to have perfect peace, what constitutes love, joy, how to develop an eternal perspective, and what to do when tempted. The Bible teaches about adultery, how to overcome anger, lust, greed, pride, hatred, bitterness, jealousy, resentment, forgiveness, how to pray, how not to pray, what constitutes holiness, happiness, humility etc.

According to the *Naves Topical Bible*, there are more than 20,000 sub topics addressed in the Bible. In other words, you can discover what God says about each of those topics. The point is, God wrote a book to teach man how to live successfully, and how to have eternal life in heaven. The Bible is the owner's manual on life. Isn't that what you would expect from a book if God wrote one? The Bible also has the exclusive and complete story of Jesus.

The Person And Work Of Jesus Christ

There is no other person in history who can claim that his coming was the fulfillment of numerous prophecies written hundreds and even thousands of years before His appearance. Jesus stands alone.

1. The prophets foretold His coming.

The Old Testament prophesied His coming in stunningly detailed predictions. Scholars tell us there are some 300 Messianic prophecies with reference to the coming of Christ as the Savior of the world. This would include but not be limited to: His lineage, His birthplace, the time, His purpose, His sacrificial death for sin, how He would die, His resurrection and many more details, hundreds and even thousands of years in advance! There is no other person in history who can make such a claim. Why such a grand entrance? So you can know you've got the right God! Imposters abound.

2. He would be born of a virgin.

In Isaiah 7:14 (written 700 years before the blessed event) under the inspiration of the Spirit of God, Isaiah wrote,

> "Therefore the Lord Himself will give you a sign: behold, a virgin will be with child and bear a son, and she will call His name Immanuel."

In this case, "Immanuel" was actually a title which meant, "God with us." The same idea is found in Revelation 19:16,

> "And on His robe and on His thigh He has a name written, KING OF KINGS, AND LORD OF LORDS."

King of Kings and Lord of Lords is more of a title than a name.

3. This child would be God in a human body.

In Isaiah 9:6 we read,

> "For a child will be born to us, a son will be given to us; and the government will rest on His shoulders; and His name will be called Wonderful Counselor, Mighty God, Eternal Father, Prince of Peace. There will be no end to the increase of {His} government or of peace, on the throne of David and over his kingdom, to establish it and to uphold it with justice and righteousness from then on and forevermore. The zeal of the LORD of hosts will accomplish this."

In Colossians 1:15 the Bible says,

> "And He (Jesus) is the image (the physical manifestation) of the invisible God, the first-born (a Hebrew idiom meaning pre-eminent) of all creation. For by Him all things were created, {both} in the heavens and on earth, visible and invisible, whether thrones or dominions or rulers or authorities-- all things have been created by Him and for Him. And He is before all things, and in Him all things hold together."

Then in John 1:1 God's Word says,

> "In the beginning was the Word, and the Word was with God, and the Word was God. He was in the beginning with God. All things came into being by Him, and apart from Him nothing came into being that has come into being. In Him was life, and the life was the light of men."

And in verse 14 of the same chapter we find this,

> "And the Word became flesh, and dwelt among us, and we beheld His glory, glory as of the only begotten from the Father, full of grace and truth."

4. The place of His birth.

The prophet Micah, writing 500 years before the fact, eliminated all the cities of the world and said the Messiah would be born in Bethlehem. Micah also reveals the Messiahs pre-existence!

"But as for you, Bethlehem Ephrathah, {too} little to be among the clans of Judah, from you One will go forth for me to be ruler in Israel. His goings forth are from long ago, from the days of eternity."

5. His family lineage.

The Messiah would be Jewish, a direct descendent of Abraham, Isaac and Jacob (Genesis 12:1-3, 28:10-15), from the Tribe of Judah (Genesis 49:10), from the family of King David (Isaiah 9:7), and be born in Bethlehem (Micah 5:2)!

6. His Sinless Life.

Is there anyone else in history who claimed to be without sin? Jesus did! This claim was also made about Him by His closest friends, relatives and by His most bitter enemies.

Peter said, "He committed no sin" (I Peter 2:22) and John said, "In Him is no sin" (I John 3:5). Judas said, "I have betrayed innocent blood" (Matthew 27:4). Pilate said, "I find in Him no fault at all" (John 18:38). The thief on the cross said, "This man has done nothing wrong" (Luke 23:41). Paul said, "He knew no sin" (2 Corinthians 5:21). Jesus said concerning Himself, "Which one of you convicts me of sin?" (John 8:46). Jesus also said, "The Father hath not left me alone; for I do always those things that please Him" (John 8:29). He was the Lamb of God without spot or blemish (1 Peter 1:19). Jesus Christ is the only person in the history of the world who never sinned.

7. His unparalleled ministry of teaching and miracles.

Isaiah said, "...the Spirit of the LORD will rest on Him, the spirit of wisdom and understanding, the spirit of counsel and strength, the spirit of knowledge and the fear of the LORD" (11:2). He would give sight to the blind and set the captives free (Isaiah 42:6-7). Jesus Himself said this prophecy was fulfilled in Luke 4:18,

> "The Spirit of the Lord is upon Me, because He anointed me to preach the gospel to the poor. He has sent me to proclaim release to the captives, and recovery of sight to the blind, to set free those who are downtrodden, To proclaim the favorable year of the Lord."

Truly, no man has ever spoken such words of love, wisdom, or life changing power before or since Jesus. His words are incomparably superior to those of any other prophet, priest or king.

The Bible tells the story of when the religious leaders of the day sent the temple guards to arrest Jesus. They returned without Him. Here is what they had to say after hearing Him speak, recorded in John 7:45-46,

> "The officers therefore came to the chief priests and Pharisees, and they said to them, 'Why did you not bring Him?' The officers answered, 'Never did a man speak the way this man speaks.'"

See *Appendix Three* to read the words of Jesus Himself in, *The Sermon on the Mount* and some of the greatest essays ever written on His life.

As The French Skeptic Ernest Renan Admitted,

> "It would take a Jesus to forge a Jesus, and if it is true that what we have in the Bible is a giant forgery, then let us worship the individual who was so brilliant as to think up a picture of a person like Jesus of Nazareth and the story of the Word of God."

James T. Fisher from: *A Few Buttons Missing: The Case Book of a Psychiatrist*:

"If you were to take the sum total of all authoritative articles ever written by the most qualified of psychologists and psychiatrists on the subject of mental hygiene, if you were to combine them and refine them and cleave out all the excess verbiage, if you were to take the whole of the meat and none of the parsley, and if you were to have these unadulterated bits of scientific knowledge concisely expressed by the most capable of living poets, you would have an awkward and incomplete summary of the Sermon on the Mount. And it would suffer immeasurably by comparison."

8. His death would be by crucifixion.

Psalm 22 was written 1,000 years before crucifixion was invented by the Romans. Verses 16-18 provide a vivid description of exactly what happened on that fateful day,

"For dogs have surrounded me; a band of evildoers has encompassed me; they pierced my hands and my feet. I can count all my bones. They look, they stare at me; They divide my garments among them, and for my clothing they cast lots."

Now compare that to John 19:23-24,

"The soldiers therefore, when they had crucified Jesus, took His outer garments and made four parts, a part to every soldier and {also} the tunic; now the tunic was seamless, woven in one piece.

They said therefore to one another, 'Let us not tear it, but cast lots for it, {to decide} whose it shall be'; that the Scripture might be fulfilled, 'They divided My outer garments among them, and for My clothing they cast lots'".

9. His suffering and death would be the payment for sin.

Isaiah 53 is the one of the most prominent Messianic prophecies in the Old Testament. It speaks of the atoning death of Jesus in stunning detail.

"He was despised and forsaken of men, a man of sorrows, and acquainted with grief; and like one from whom men hide their face, He was despised, and we did not esteem Him. Surely our griefs He himself bore, and our sorrows He carried;

yet we ourselves esteemed Him stricken, smitten of God, and afflicted."

"But He was pierced through for our transgressions, He was crushed for our iniquities; the chastening for our well-being {fell} upon Him, and by His scourging we are healed." (Isaiah 53: 1-4).

"He was oppressed and He was afflicted, yet He did not open His mouth; like a lamb that is led to slaughter, and like a sheep that is silent before its shearers, so He did not open His mouth."

"By oppression and judgment He was taken away; and as for His generation, who considered that He was cut off out of the land of the living, for the transgression of my people to whom the stroke {was due?} His grave was assigned with wicked men, yet He was with a rich man in His death, because He had done no violence, nor was there any deceit in His mouth." (Isaiah 53:7-9).

10. His resurrection.

Psalms 16:9-10, "Therefore my heart is glad, and my glory rejoices; My flesh also will dwell securely. For Thou wilt not abandon my soul to Sheol; neither wilt Thou allow Thy Holy One to undergo decay."

The following quote is one of the most compelling legal arguments ever offered on the resurrection of Jesus Christ. Professor Simon Greenleaf was asked by his law students to give his expert opinion on the resurrection, was it true or not? After a thorough examination of the New Testament, Simon Greenleaf not only wrote a book on the subject, but he surrendered his life to the Lord Jesus Christ. Simon Greenleaf was Jewish, and after critically examining the testimony of the Apostles, realized that Jesus Christ *was* and *is* the promised Messiah of the Old Testament.

"Simon Greenleaf was the famous Royal Professor of Law at Harvard University and succeeded Justice Joseph Story as the Dane Professor of Law in the same university, upon Story's death. H. W. H. Knott says of this great authority in jurisprudence: "To the efforts of Story and Greenleaf is to be ascribed the rise of the Harvard Law School to its eminent position among the legal schools of the United States.

"While still a Professor of Law at Harvard University, Greenleaf produced a famous work entitled: *A Treatise on the Law of Evidence* which is still considered the greatest single authority on evidence in the entire literature of legal procedure.

"Greenleaf also wrote a volume entitled: *An Examination of the Testimony of the Four Evangelists by the Rules of Evidence Administered in the Courts of Justice.* What you are about to read is the opinion of one of the world's foremost leading authorities on what constitutes good evidence in a court of law concerning the Apostles' claim that Jesus was actually resurrected from the dead,

> 'The great truths which the apostles declared were that Christ had risen from the dead, and that only through repentance from sin and faith in Him, could men hope for salvation. This doctrine they asserted with one voice, everywhere, not only under the greatest discouragements, but in the face of the most appalling errors that can be presented to the mind of man. Their master had recently perished as a malefactor, by the sentence of a public tribunal. His religion sought to overthrow the religions of the whole world. The laws of every country were against the teachings of His disciples. The interests and passions of all the rulers and great men in the world were against them. The fashion of the world was against them. Propagating this new faith, even in the most inoffensive and peaceful manner, they could expect nothing but contempt, opposition, revilings, bitter persecutions, stripes, imprisonments, torments, and cruel deaths. Yet this faith they zealously did propagate; and all these miseries they endured undismayed, nay, rejoicing. As one after another was put to a miserable death, the survivors only prosecuted their work with increased vigor and resolution. The annals of military warfare afford scarcely an example of the like heroic constancy, patience, and unblenching courage. They had every possible motive to review carefully the grounds of their faith, and the evidences of the great facts and truths which they asserted; and these motives were pressed upon their attention with the most melancholy and terrific frequency. It was therefore impossible that they could have persisted in affirming

the truths they have narrated, had not Jesus actually risen from the dead." [1]

11. His influence for the last 2,000 years and forever.

Isaiah 9:7, "There will be no end to the increase of {His} government or of peace, On the throne of David and over his kingdom, to establish it and to uphold it with justice and righteousness from then on and forevermore. The zeal of the LORD of hosts will accomplish this."

Here is what Malcolm Muggeridge had to say about Jesus and His influence,

"We look back upon history and what do we see? Empires rising and falling, revolutions and counter-revolutions, wealth accumulating and wealth dispersed, one nation dominant and then another. Shakespeare speaks of 'the rise and fall of great ones that ebb and flow with the moon.' I look back on my own fellow countrymen ruling over a quarter of the world, the great majority of them convinced, in the words of what is still a favorite song, that, 'God who's made the mighty, would make them mightier yet.' I've heard a crazed, cracked Austrian announce to the world the establishment of a German Reich that would last a thousand years; an Italian clown announce that he would restart the calendar to begin his own ascension to power. I've heard a murderous Georgian brigand in the Kremlin acclaimed by the intellectual elite of the world as a wiser than Solomon, more humane than Marcus Aurelius, more enlightened than Ashoka.

"I've seen America wealthier and in terms of weaponry, more powerful than the rest of the world put together, so that had the American people desired, could have outdone an Alexander or a Julius Caesar in the range and scale of their conquests. All in one lifetime, all in one lifetime, all gone with the wind. England, part of a tiny island off the coast of Europe, threatened with dismemberment and even bankruptcy. Hitler and Mussolini dead, remembered only in infamy. Stalin, a forbidden name in the regime he helped found and dominate for some three decades. America, haunted by fears of running out of those precious fluids that keep her motorways roaring, and the smog settling, with troubled memories of a disastrous campaign in Vietnam, and the victories of the Don Quixotes of the media as they charged the windmills of Watergate. All in one lifetime, all gone, gone with the wind. Behind the debris of these self-styled, sullen supermen and imperial diplomats, there stands the gigantic figure of one person, because of whom, by whom, in whom, and through whom alone mankind might still have hope, the person of Jesus Christ." [2]

Christianity Is Christ

Virtually all other religions are based on the philosophies of their founders. Islam is based on the teaching of one man, Mohammed. Buddhism is based on the philosophy of Buddha. Confucianism is based on the beliefs of Confucius, and so it goes. Christianity is based not only on the teaching of Jesus, but on Christ Himself.

If you take Mohammed out of Islam, the basic tenants of Islam would not change. You don't need Mohammed in *any personal way* in order to be a Muslim. If you take Buddha out of Buddhism, the teachings of Buddha remain the same. If you take Confucius out of Confucianism, they will be just as confused as they were before. But if you take Christ out of Christianity, there is nothing left.

Jesus is not just our Redeemer, He is our redemption. Jesus is not just our Savior, He is our salvation. Jesus does not just teach us how to be sanctified, He *is* our sanctification!

Since all other religions are merely the opinions of men, they are subjective, and no matter how appealing their teaching may be to our felt needs, or how one may be pressured by culture to accept these religions as true, that does not make them right.

The Resurrection

The most profound demonstration of God's love for mankind is revealed in the death and the resurrection of Jesus Christ. It was His sacrifice that made atonement for sin and provided redemption not only for man, but for the universe itself. Yes, even the universe is dying. Physicists call it the Second Law of Thermal Dynamics. Theologians know what it's called and what causes it; it's called sin. The Bible says that God is going to let sin run its course. After that, He will create new heavens and a new earth where righteousness dwells-forever!

The cross of Christ represents the defining moment in the history of mankind. Jesus had such a profound impact on the world by what He said and by what He did that the world marks time before His birth and after His death. We live in the 21st century "A.D". That is Latin for Anno Domini which means "In the year of the Lord". The reason the world marks time by the birth and death of Jesus is because three days after He was crucified, He raised Himself from the dead! No one ever did that before or since.

I'm not so amazed that Jesus raised Himself from the dead. I'm more amazed that He could have died in the first place! Death is the result of sin. That is why all men die, no matter how they die. But Jesus was sinless. How could He have died? The answer is found in 2 Corinthians 5:21,

> "He made Him who knew no sin {to be} sin on our behalf, that we might become the righteousness of God in Him."

Christ died all right—He took on the sins of the whole world, past, present and future! That is how God can legally forgive us without compromising His justice. Someone else paid the price for you!

According to the New Testament, repentance and believing in the deity of Jesus is what constitutes salvation. In John 8:26 Jesus said,

> "... you shall die in your sins; for unless you believe that I am (He) you shall die in your sins."

John 1:1 and Colossians 1:17 state that Jesus was God manifested in human flesh, eternal and not created. Anyone can say that he or she is a prophet, anyone can say, "I am God", but proving it is much more difficult. There are seven "I am" sayings of Jesus in the New Testament. Each is a clear reference to Exodus 3:14 when God revealed His name to Moses: "I am, that I am, tell them I am." So, when Jesus said, "Before Abraham was, I Am," the Pharisees knew exactly what He meant, and they wanted to stone Him for claiming to be God (John 8:58, 59; 10:30,31)!

Talk Is Cheap

Jesus said, "I am the light of the world". But, He did not just *say*, "I am the light of the world," He *said*, "I am the light of the world" and He gave sight to a man born blind! He said, "I am the bread of life." But He did not just *say*, "I am the bread of life," He *said*, "I am the bread of life", and He fed 5,000 people with a few loaves of bread and a couple of fish! He did not just *say*, "I am the resurrection and the life." He *said*, "I am the resurrection and the life" and He raised Lazarus (and many others) from the dead!

Each of the "I Am" sayings was accompanied by a miracle, which in turn revealed His deity. The one miracle He performed more than any other was that of giving sight to the blind. In Exodus 4:11, God is speaking to Moses,

> "And the LORD said to him, 'Who has made man's mouth? Or who makes {him} dumb or deaf, or seeing or blind? Is it not I, the LORD?'"

The "I Am" sayings show that Jesus not only claimed to be God, but offered empirical proof of being the Creator, the Sustainer, and the Redeemer of mankind. He proved His verbal claims with literal miracles. Jesus said, "Peace be still" and the winds and the sea obeyed Him! He said, "Destroy this temple and in three days I will raise it." He was speaking of the temple of His body!

Jesus claimed to be God. He not only said He was God (anyone can *say* that), He offered proof of His claim by doing things only God could do. If God came to earth as a man, you would expect Him to say and do things that would clearly distinguish Him from all other men. Jesus did!

No Greater Love

Another outstanding basis for proof that the Bible is divinely inspired is its unparalleled teaching on love. How is this proof of divinity? We are social creatures. God made us that way. One of man's greatest needs is to love and be loved. The Bible reveals the most comprehensive teaching on love that there is.

The word love is defined, explained, illustrated, exemplified, proved and demonstrated hundreds of times in the Bible. The number of times the word is used is not the point. The fact is, you cannot find a more comprehensive teaching on love in any other religion, philosophy or system of thought. Not even close. Love is more than an emotion, it's proactive and it's powerful enough to soften the hardest heart when nothing else will. Love is one of the attributes of God.

Christianity is not a religion, it's a revelation. And once you have had the revelation, it leads you to a personal love relationship with God. It is both the law of God and the love of God that draws us to Christ. Our relationship with God is based on faith, hope and love in and through the Lord Jesus Christ.

If everyone loved God and loved their neighbors as themselves we would live in a perfect world! The opposite of love is not just hate, it's also selfishness. For God so loved the world He gave! Selfishness is the essence of sin, and giving is the fruit of love. Man will never solve his own problems because man *is* the problem. Man (without God) is inherently selfish.

No one has ever taken love to the level Jesus did. It was Christ who said, "Love your enemies." But He didn't just *say*, "Love your enemies." He *said*, "Love your enemies", and while He hung on the cross, in unimaginable pain from the top of His head to the tips of His toes, He prayed, "Father forgive them for they know not what they do." No mere man has ever loved like that. This love was so profound, so completely antithetical to human nature, the thief on his right recognized His divinity, and said, "Lord, remember me when you come into your kingdom." Jesus replied, "This day you shall be with Me in Paradise." No one could make up such stories and expect anyone to believe them.

The greatest commandment in the Bible is to love God and love our neighbors as ourselves (Matthew 22:36-40). God is love (1 John 4:8). For God so loved the world He gave His only begotten Son (John 3:16). We love God because He first loved us (1 John 4:19). To love God you must love your brother (1 John 4:20). If you mistreat your wife your prayers are hindered (1 Peter 3:7). Love is defined (1 Corinthians 13: 1-8). We are obligated to love (Romans 13:1-8). Sacrificial love is the key to a happy marriage (Ephesians 5:25). There is no greater love than to sacrifice your life to save a friend (John 15:13). Love is the distinguishing mark of the Christian (John 13:35). True love is unconditional (Luke 6:32). Love includes your enemies (Luke 6:27). Love is the greatest spiritual gift (1 Corinthians 13: 13). Obedience to God is based on love (John 14:15). God demonstrates His own love toward us, in that while we were yet sinners, Christ died for us (Romans 5:8). There are hundreds more.

How Powerful Is The Love Of Jesus?

"I know men, and I tell you that Jesus Christ is no mere man. Between Him and every other person in the world there is no possible term of comparison. Alexander, Caesar, Charlemagne, and I founded empires. But on what did we rest the creations of our genius? Upon force. Jesus Christ founded His empire upon love; and at this hour millions of people would die for Him."

—Napoleon Bonaparte

A Closing Illustration On The Power Of Love

"Rabbi Michael Weisser lived in Lincoln, Nebraska. And for more than 3 years, Larry Trapp, a self-proclaimed Nazi & Ku Klux Klansman, directed a torrent of hate-filled mailings & phone calls toward him.

"Trapp promoted white supremacy, anti-Semitism, & other messages of prejudice, declaring his apartment the KKK state headquarters & himself the Grand Dragon. His whole purpose in life seemed to be to spew out hate-ridden racial slurs & obscene remarks against Weisser & all those like him.

"At first, the Weissers; were so afraid they locked their doors & worried themselves almost sick over the safety of their family.

"But one day Rabbi Weisser found out that Trapp was a 42-year-old clinically blind, double amputee. And he became convinced that Trapp's own physical helplessness was a source of the bitterness he expressed.

"So Rabbi Weisser decided to do the unexpected. He left a message on Trapp's answering machine, telling him of another side of life ... a life free of hatred & racism. Rabbi Weisser said, 'I probably called 10 times & left messages before he finally picked up the phone & asked me why I was harassing him. I said that I'd like to help him. I offered him a ride to the grocery store or to the mall.

"Trapp was stunned. Disarmed by the kindness & courtesy, he started thinking. He later admitted, through tears, that he heard in the rabbi's voice, 'something I hadn't experienced in years. It was love.

"Slowly the bitter man began to soften. One night he called the Weissrs, & said he wanted out, but didn't know how. They grabbed a bucket of fried chicken & took him dinner. Before long they made a trade: in return for their love he gave them his swastika rings, hate tracts, & Klan robes.

"That same day Trapp gave up his Ku Klux Klan recruiting job & dumped the rest of his propaganda in the trash. 'They showed me so much love that I couldn't help but love them back,' he finally confessed."[3]

A Final Thought

If that is what a simple act of kindness can do to a Nazi and a Ku Klux Klansman from Lincoln, Nebraska, what would happen if we practiced the same kind of sacrificial love that Jesus exemplified in our own homes and neighborhoods?

End Notes

1. My thanks to Josh McDowell's, *Evidence that Demands a Verdict.*

2. Malcolm Muggeridge.

3. This story is by Melvin Newland from Sermon Central.

Small Group Questions

1. Why should we believe the Bible?

2. How is the Bible different from other so-called 'holy books'?

3. How do we know that the Ten Commandments are divinely inspired?

4. Read Matthew 5:21-22. What is Jesus teaching us about the 6th commandment?

5. Read Matthew 5:27-28. What is Jesus teaching us about the 7th commandment?

6. Simon Greenleaf became a Christian after reading the Gospel accounts. What was it that convinced him that Jesus was who He claimed to be and the Bible was true?

7. Malcolm Muggeridge became a Christian after studying Christianity. What convinced him?

8. The Temple guards said no man ever spoke like Jesus. What are some of the things He said that are so profound?

9. What are some of the things Jesus did that only God can do?

Chapter Three

How Can One God Be a Trinity?

Is the Trinity a blatant contradiction? Do Christians really worship three gods as the cultists claim? The Trinity is one of the most misunderstood and frequently attacked doctrines by the cults and false religions.

Unfortunately, when it comes to the Trinity, the average cultist can twist the average Christian into a theological pretzel in less than a minute. Christians who believe in this biblical doctrine are labeled by the cults as polytheists. On the surface, the Trinity does appear to be a difficult doctrine. In reality, there are tri-unities all around us that we can comprehend perfectly.

Admittedly, the word Trinity is not found in the Bible, so where do we get this idea from? It actually begins in the very first verse of the Bible. Genesis 1:1 says, "In the beginning God created the heavens and the earth."

In Genesis 1:1 the Hebrew the word translated "God" is Elohim—Elohim is the *plural* form of "El" which means God. If Genesis 1:1 were translated literally in English it would read, "In the beginning *Gods* created the heavens and the earth! Rest assured that God does not need lessons in Hebrew grammar. Nor is He afraid of being misinterpreted. He means what He says and He says what He means!

The translators may have been afraid that uneducated people might get the wrong idea so they digested the word for us and *interpreted* in the singular rather than *translating* it in the plural. Our next clue is found in the very next verse. Genesis 1:2 reads, "And the earth was formless and void, and darkness was over the surface of the deep; and the Spirit of God was moving over the surface of the waters."

First we have "Gods" creating the heavens and the Earth, and then we discover the Spirit of God moving over the surface of the waters. Then in Genesis 1:26 we read, "God said, "Let Us make man in Our image, according to Our likeness…""

The question is, to whom is God speaking when He says (three times) "Let *Us* make man in *Our* image and according to *Our* likeness" (italics added)? The grammar in this verse reveals at least two persons. But the audience could not have been the angels. As created beings themselves, they do not have the power to create.

Now let's look at a fascinating verse in Isaiah 48:12: "Listen to me, O Jacob, even Israel whom I called; I am He, I am the first, I am also the last. Surely My hand founded the earth, and My right hand spread out the heavens; when I call to them, they stand together." Jumping down to verse 16, we read: "Come near to me, listen to this: from the first I have not spoken in secret, from the time it took place, I was there. And now the Lord GOD has sent me, and His Spirit."

Notice that last verse, "And now *the Lord GOD* (the word LORD is YHWH in Hebrew and refers to God the Father) has sent *me* (that is Jesus speaking. In Revelation 22:13-16 Jesus is identified as 'the First and the Last)' and His Spirit (that is the Holy Spirit)." There you have the Trinity all in one verse, in the Old Testament!

Here is another great example from Proverbs 30:4: "Who has ascended into heaven and descended? Who has gathered the wind in His fists? Who has wrapped the waters in His garment? Who has established all the ends of the earth? What is His name or His son's name? Surely you know!"

We *know* the answer to this riddle. His name is YHWH and His Son's name is YSHUA (Jesus)! There are many more such references in the Old Testament and at least 50 more in the New Testament. We will look at just one to make our point. This example is found in Matthew 3:16-17,

> "And after being baptized, Jesus went up immediately from the water; and behold, the heavens were opened, and he saw the Spirit of God descending as a dove, {and} coming upon

Him, and behold, a voice out of the heavens, saying, 'This is My beloved Son, in whom I am well-pleased.'"

Illustrating The Trinity

The fact is creation itself is filled with illustrations of spiritual truths that reveal the many attributes of God, one of which is the Trinity. For example, Einstein's theory of relativity provides the basis for understanding that life as we know it consists of three things: time, space, and matter (which is energy).

Interestingly, the Bible starts with, "In the beginning, God created the heavens and the earth." In the beginning (that's time), God created (that's energy), the heavens (that's space), and the earth (that's matter)!

Time: Time is a trinity. It has three elements: the past, the present and the future. The past is not the present, the present is not the future, and the future is not the past. One is not the other, all are part of the same, none can exist without the other, and yet each is distinct!

Space: We live in a three-dimensional world, height, width, and depth. Height is not width, width is not depth and depth is not height. One is not the other, all are part of the same, none can exist without the other, and yet each is distinct!

Matter: All matter is made up of atoms. All atoms consist of three basic components: protons, neutrons and electrons. A proton is not a neutron, a neutron is not an electron, and an electron is not a proton. One is not the other, all are part of the same, none can exist without the other (being a complete atom), and yet each one is distinct! 1

The Nature Of Man

Genesis tells us that man is made in the image of God. In 1 Thessalonians 5:23 the Bible says, "Now may the God of peace Himself sanctify you entirely; and may your spirit and soul and body be preserved complete, without blame at the coming of our Lord Jesus Christ." According to this verse, each of us has a triune nature consisting of a body, a soul, and a spirit. In the original Greek language of the New Testament the word body is *soma*, the word for soul is *psuche*, and the word for spirit is *pneuma*. Your soma is not your psuche, your psuche is not your pneuma and your pneuma is not your soma. One is not the other, all are part of the same, none can exist without the other, and yet each one is distinct!

The Human Mind

Scientists tell us that the human mind is the most complex thing in the universe. The mind is also a trinity—the mind, the will, and the emotions. Your mind, (intellect) is not the same as your emotions. Your emotions are not the same as your will. Your will is not the same as your intellect. One is not the other, all are part of the same, none can exist without the other, and yet each one is distinct!

Insights From Light

When Einstein discovered the theory of relativity, he was trying to answer the question, "What is light?" Interestingly, in 1 John 1:5 the Bible says, "And this is the message we have heard from Him and announce to you, that God is light, and in Him there is no darkness at all."

We do not know if this verse is speaking strictly metaphorically, referring to God's perfect holiness, or if God actually is light (or both), but fascinating parallels exist between the triune nature of God and what we know about light. Specifically we know there is invisible light, visible light and the heat associated with light.

The Father

Invisible light includes infrared, ultraviolet, and others such as microwaves, radio waves, X-rays, gamma rays. These forms of light are invisible to the human eye. This type of light is neither seen nor felt.

In 1 Timothy 1:17 the Bible says God the Father is invisible:

"Now to the King eternal, immortal, invisible, the only God, {be} honor and glory forever and ever."

The same idea is found in John 4:24:

"God is spirit and those who worship Him must worship in spirit and in truth."

The Son

Secondly, there is thermal light such as the light of the sun or the light from an incandescent light bulb. This type of light is both seen and felt!

John 1:1 speaks of Jesus:

> "In the beginning was the Word, and the Word was with God, and the Word was God." Then, John 1:14 says, "And the word became flesh, and we beheld His glory."

Clearly this verse tells us that Jesus was both seen and felt. Then we have I John 1:1-3, speaking again of Jesus,

> "What was from the beginning, what we have heard, what we have seen with our eyes, what we beheld and our hands handled, concerning the Word of Life—and the life was manifested, and we have seen and bear witness and proclaim to you the eternal life, which was with the Father and was manifested to us—what we have seen and heard we proclaim to you also, that you also may have fellowship with us; and indeed our fellowship is with the Father, and with His Son Jesus Christ."

The Holy Spirit

Then we have the heat associated with light. In Matthew 3:11 we read,

> "…He who is coming after me is mightier than I, and I am not fit to remove His sandals; He will baptize you with the Holy Spirit and fire."

And in Acts 2:2-4, again the Holy Spirit is associated with fire:

> "And suddenly there came from heaven a noise like a violent, rushing wind, and it filled the whole house where they were sitting. And there appeared to them tongues as of fire distributing themselves, and they rested on each one of them. And they were all filled with the Holy Spirit and began to speak with other tongues, as the Spirit was giving them utterance."

I am not saying these facts about light are perfect illustrations of the Trinity and I am not trying to be sensational. I am saying that these are fascinating parallels. What I am trying to show is that the Trinity is not an unfathomable, illogical, irreconcilable, contradiction—there are tri-unities all around us.

Whether or not you can rationally understand something does not preclude you from believing it. I do not understand atomic theory. But that does not prevent me from enjoying the benefits of the electricity that flows from our nuclear power plants. But for those who are still adamant that God cannot be a Trinity, how a mortal man, who has never seen God and cannot even begin to comprehend His nature, can insist that God cannot be a Trinity is more of a mystery to me than the Trinity itself!

Why is the Trinity even important? If the critics are right, then the Trinity *is* a contradiction and a damnable heresy. But the exact opposite is true if Jesus was right when He said in John 8:24, "Unless you believe I Am (*God*), you will die in your sin!"

A Closing Illustration

It was a Saturday afternoon. I was in a Mexican restaurant with 10 volunteers from our prison ministry. We were having a great time celebrating life and a fruitful ministry. We were laughing and having a good time when four men walked in and sat right behind us. They were speaking a foreign language and were louder than we were. My wife, who is as bold as a lion, turned around and asked, "Excuse me, are you speaking Farsi?"

They said, "Yes, how did you know?"

She said, "I have an Assyrian and an Armenian background." Usually, when an Assyrian or an Armenian meets another person with that ethnic background, they get all excited and are ready to jump up and start dancing in a circle holding handkerchiefs, but not in this case. My wife turned back to me, leaned forward and whispered, "They're Muslims!"

I said, "nahhhh."

She said, "Oh yes they are!"

So without even thinking (which is usually when I'm at my best) I said to these men, "Gentlemen, excuse me." They turned around, and I said, "I'm sorry to bother you, I'm just curious, are you guys Muslims?"

The first said, "Yes." The second would not speak, the third said he was "undecided," and the fourth said, in a voice so loud the whole restaurant could hear him, "I am a Darwinian evolutionist, a socialist, and a follower of Adolph Hitler." He then went into a monologue about all of the wonderful attributes of socialism!

So I got up, put my sport coat on, walked around our table, walked right up to this man and said, "Sir, there are three reasons no man will stand before God with any excuse for ignoring or denying Him. First of all, all a thinking person has to do is take a good look at the sun, the moon and the stars to know that anything so complex, so well ordered, so perfectly designed and well balanced as is our world and our universe and your own human body, which is fearfully and wonderfully made, could in no way have made itself. The Bible says, "Only a fool would say, 'there is no God.'"

The second reason no man will stand before God with any excuse is because of the Word. The written Word is the Bible and the Living Word which is Jesus Christ. I can prove that the Bible is true with one word—Israel. The Bible says, in the book of Ezekiel, written 2,500 years ago that Israel would be destroyed as a nation, because of her sin, they would be exiled from the land, and that land would remain desolate for a long, long time. Then in the Last days God would bring them back into the land. That is exactly what happened.

In A.D. 70, Titus and the Roman Army destroyed Jerusalem and the Jews ran to the 4 corners of the earth. It was not until then end of World War II when Hitler was stopped that the Jews began to trickle back into the land. Then in 1948, Israel was declared a nation again precisely as the Bible predicted.

And as for Jesus, Napoleon said, "I know men, and I tell you that Jesus Christ is no mere man. Between Him and every other person there is no possible term of comparison. Cesar, Alexander, Charlemagne and I have all founded empires, but on what did we base our genius? Upon force. Jesus Christ founded His empire on love and today, millions are willing to die for Him."

The third reason no man will stand before God with any excuse for ignoring or denying Him is right inside your own chest. Romans 2:15 says, "The law is written on every man's heart." Every man from the beginning of time until the end of the world knows in his heart, it is wrong to murder, it's wrong to steal, it's wrong to lie, it's wrong to have another man's wife. Every man knows there is a God in heaven because the sun and the moon and the stars declare His glory. And you know it's true, and I know you know it's true and God knows you know it's true, isn't that true?"

He jumped up out of his seat, stuck his hand out, and smiling from ear to ear, said, "If I was going to choose a religion, I would choose Christianity!" And he shook my hand!

I looked at my wife and said, "Do you have the Muslim tracts? Give me the Muslim tracts! She reached in her purse and pulled out four little booklets that compare Christianity to Islam, and all four men took one and said, "Thank you."

A Final Thought

When it comes to sharing the Gospel, God did not leave us to fend for ourselves. He left us a perfect systematic theology of evangelism that cannot be improved upon by any man. Just as mathematics is a perfect science, so is presenting the Gospel.

The Trinity has been a stumbling-block for many. However, as you can see the Trinity can be explained in a manner that makes sense. Many people have come out of the cults and the false religions after hearing or reading this teaching on the Trinity.

End Notes

I owe a debt of gratitude to Dr. Henry Morris for his excellent insights on the Trinity. His book, *Many Infallible Proofs* is well worth reading. I am also grateful for the ministry of the late great Adrian Rogers. His sermon on the Trinity is superb.

Small Group Questions

1.   Was there anything in this chapter that intrigued you, and if so, what was it, and why?

2.   How is time a trinity? How is space a trinity? How is matter a trinity?

3.   Compare Exodus 3:14 to John 8:24. What is Jesus saying in this verse? Also see John 10:30. Who does Jesus say that He is?

4.   In this light, why is the Trinity important?

5.   The word *Trinity* is not found in the Bible. Where do we see the Trinity in the Bible?

6.   How is the human mind a trinity?

7.   What are the parallels between light and the Trinity?

8.   Do I have to completely understand something before I can believe it's true? Why?

9.   How is love a trinity?

10. Can you think of any other tri-unities?

Chapter Four

Isn't Evolution a Proven Scientific Fact?

A better question might be, "If evolution *is* a proven scientific fact, why are so many of the world's leading scientists speaking out against the so-called "evidence" for evolution? Some of the finest minds in the world have labeled it everything from "Monkey Mythology" to "the greatest hoax in history!" (For a list of more than 700 Ph.D.s who have signed a petition boldly stating that they disagree with Darwin's theory, go to this website for more information: www.dissentfromdarwin.org).

If there are 700 scientific 'prophets' who are not afraid to come out of the closet, that means there are many more who also disagree with evolution but are afraid to state their views publicly for various reasons, such as the fear of losing their jobs. This sad fact has been well documented by Ben Stein, a secular researcher, whose film documentary *Expelled* did an outstanding job of exposing the censorship, the bias, and the outright suppression of the mountains of evidence that exist for intelligent design. I highly recommend this excellent DVD.

Contrary to popular opinion, the fact of the matter is, Macro-Evolution (the process by which one species becomes another) has never been observed in a laboratory (or anywhere else, for that matter)!

In Darwin's Own Words

Since Charles Darwin is 'put on a pedestal' by virtually all who claim to accept the idea of spontaneous evolution, his thoughts and comments are very relevant to this discussion. Far from unquestioningly accepting the idea of macroevolution, Darwin posed these questions himself:

"Why, if species have descended from other species by insensibly fine gradations, do we not everywhere see innumerable transitional forms? Why is not all nature in confusion instead of the species being, as we see them, well defined?" [1]

"According to this theory, innumerable transitional forms must have existed; why do we not find them embedded in countless numbers in the crust of the earth?" [2]

"Lastly, looking not to any one time, but to all time, if the theory is true, numberless intermediate varieties, linking closely together all the species of the same group, must assuredly have existed." [3]

"Why then is not every geological formation and every stratum full of such intermediate links? Geology assuredly does not reveal any such finely graduated organic chain; and this, perhaps, is the most obvious and gravest objection which can be urged against the theory." [4]

Darwin went on to say something even more ironic:

"He who rejects this view of the imperfection of the geological record will rightly reject the whole theory." [5]

Did you catch that? In Darwin's own words, if his theory of evolution were true, we would see a vast number of fossils at intermediate stages of biological development. If we do not, then *we are right to reject the whole theory*!

And What Does The Fossil Record Show?

"Author Luther Sunderland interviewed five respected museum officials, recognized authorities in their individual fields of study, including representatives from the American Museum, the Field Museum of Natural History in Chicago, and the British Museum of Natural History. None of the five officials were able to offer a single example of a transitional series of fossilized organisms that document the transformation of one kind of plant or animal into another.

"One interviewee was Dr. Colin Patterson (Senior Paleontologist at the British Museum of Natural History and editor of a prestigious scientific journal). Since the British Museum has the largest fossil collection in the world, Dr. Patterson had ample opportunity to hone his well-known expertise in knowledge of the fossil record. He was unable to give a single example of macro-evolutionary transition and, in his book *Evolution* Dr. Patterson did not include a single photograph of a transitional fossil. When asked why not, he responded:

'I fully agree with your comments on the lack of direct illustration of evolutionary transitions in my book. If I knew of any I would certainly have included them. Yet [Dr. Stephen] Gould and the American Museum people are hard to contradict when they say there are no transitional fossils. As a paleontologist myself, I am much occupied with the philosophical problems of identifying ancestral forms in the fossil record. You say that I should at least 'show a photo of the fossil from which each type of organism was derived.' I will lay it on the line: there is not one such fossil for which one could make a watertight argument." [6]

We invite the reader to ask evolutionary college professors to explain how evolution can be called science when eminent scholars, whose intellectual integrity is beyond question, have gone on record with conclusions like these:

"Our museums now contain hundreds of millions of fossil specimens (40 million in the Smithsonian Natural History Museum alone). If Darwin's theory were true, we should see tens of millions of unquestionably transitional forms. We see none.

"In fact, based on standard mathematical models, we would see far more transitional forms in the fossil record than complete specimens. However, we see none; not one true transitional specimen has ever been found. You would also expect to see transitional forms walking around today. But no, all we see are fully formed animals. Dogs are dogs, cats are cats, fish are fish, and birds are birds.

"...paleontology provides...some nasty difficulties for evolutionists, the most notorious of which is the presence of 'gaps' in the fossil record. Evolution requires intermediate forms between species and paleontology does not provide them" (Dr. David Kitts, Head Curator of the Department of Geology at the Stovall Museum)

"My attempts to demonstrate evolution by an experiment carried on for more than 40 years have completely failed... The fossil material is now so complete that it has been possible to construct new classes, and the lack of transitional series cannot be explained as being due to scarcity of material. The deficiencies are real; they will never be filled." N. Heribert-Nilsson, botanist and professor at Lund University, Sweden).

"In Darwin's day, (the mid-1800s), paleontology was a new branch of science. Today, 150 years later, the fossil record proves Darwin's theory was wrong!" [2]

There you have it: the fossil record shows that evolution is nothing more than a fairy tale for adults. A common phrase used by evolutionists is that the evidence for evolution is "overwhelmingly conclusive." Absolutely nothing could be further from the truth. As G.K. Chesterton once observed,

"The evolutionist seems to know everything about the missing link except the fact that it is missing!"

What About Mutations?

"Many so-called scientists claim that mutations occur within species and, therefore, prove evolution to be true. What they don't say is that mutations are rare occurrences and, even when they occur, they rarely, if ever, have anything but negative effects on an organism.

"Evolutionists claim mutations are responsible for the evolution of simple cells into more complex organisms. Yet not one scientist has ever observed macroevolution in a laboratory. This remains true despite more than 150 years of intensive scientific research.

"Mutations involve permanent changes in a cell's DNA, but these are mistakes, not 'improvements', that result in defective protein molecules that don't function properly. These malfunctions are well known for causing genetic disorders and disease, e.g., cystic fibrosis, sickle-cell anemia, albinism, and hemophilia.

"Scientists are working fervently to create life from non-living matter in an attempt to prove evolution. But if they ever do succeed, they would only prove that it required intelligence, not random chance, to make it happen!" [7]

What Are The Real Motives Behind Atheism?

Aldous Huxley (1894–1963) was the grandson of Thomas Huxley, who was an English biologist. He was known as "Darwin's Bulldog" for his bold defense of Charles Darwin's theory of evolution. Aldous Huxley was a writer and one of the most prominent members of the famous Huxley family. Aldous Huxley, like his grandfather before him, was an outspoken atheist. In this priceless quote, he speaks for most atheists (whether they like it or not):

"I had motives for not wanting the world to have meaning; consequently assumed it had none, and was able without any difficulty to find satisfying reasons for this assumption. The philosopher who finds no meaning in the world is not concerned exclusively with a problem of pure metaphysics; he is also concerned to prove there is no valid reason why he personally should not do as he wants to do. For myself, as no doubt for most of my contemporaries, the philosophy of meaninglessness was essentially an instrument of liberation. The liberation we desired was simultaneously liberation from a certain political and economic system, and liberation from a certain system of morality. We objected to the morality because it interfered with our sexual freedom." [8]

Huxley's self-imposed spiritual blindness was not an intellectual problem; Huxley had a moral problem. It was not a matter of the mind, but of the will. If the atheist does *not* a moral problem, then unbelief is a psychological problem.

Atheists Are Not Created; They Evolve

"A study was done a while back into all the famous atheists of history, Jean Paul Sartre, Camus, Friedrich Nietzche, Sigmund Freud, Karl Marx, Madalyn Murray O'Hair, and every single one of them had something in common. They either lost their father when they were young, their father abandoned their family, or they had a terrible relationship with their father. That is very interesting because often these doubts aren't really driven by intellectual questions; they are being driven by an emotional issue that really blocks them from *wanting* to relate to a heavenly father because they feel so abandoned, or cheated, or hurt by their earthly father." [9]

A Closing Illustration

When the Russians sent the first manned rocket into space, the cosmonaut went up about 100 miles, circled the earth and returned safely. Shortly thereafter, the atheistic Russian government held a press conference. They proudly announced to the world that their man had gone up to the heavens, looked around for God and did not see Him. The obvious implication was they now had a first-hand eyewitness account that God did not exist. Well, if the cosmonaut had just gone one foot farther, he would have proven God's existence. If he just would have stepped outside of his little space capsule and shut the door behind him, he would have seen God!

A Final Thought

In reality, atheism is a crutch for those who can't bear the thought of identifying themselves with Jesus Christ and admitting they are sinners. Based on pride, the crutch will not hold when they stand before God. The truth is, God is the Creator of the universe, and all things relate back to Him. He gives meaning and purpose to *everything*!

"It is absurd for the evolutionist to complain that it is unthinkable for an admittedly unthinkable God to make everything out of nothing, and then pretend that it is more thinkable that nothing should turn itself into anything." [10]

End Notes

1. Darwin: *Origin of the Species*, p. 143.

2. Ibid., 144.

3. Ibid., 149.

4. Ibid., 230.

5. Ibid., 342.

6. Randall Niles, "*Problems with the Fossil Record,*" All About the Journey www.all-aboutthejourney.org/problems-with-the-fossil-record.html.

7. Lawrence O. Richards, *It Couldn't Just Happen* (Thomas Nelson, Inc., 1989), pp. 139-140.

8. Aldous Huxley, *Ends and Means*, 1937.

9. Lee Strobel; Radio interview on Moody Radio.

10. G. K. Chesterton—*The Quotable Chesterton*.

Small Group Questions

1. If scientists ever were able to generate life from non-living matter, far from proving evolution, what would it prove?

2. Darwin himself said if his theory were true, we would find millions of fossils showing intermediate life forms, that is, one species changing into another. Now, 150 years later, what does the fossil record show?

3. What is the difference between hypothesis and theory?

4. What is macro-evolution, and has it ever been observed in a laboratory or anywhere else?

5. What are some of the results of 150 years of Darwinian evolution on our society, in our government school systems, and in our world?

6. What would happen to our world if everyone stopped lying tomorrow? What if we stopped stealing? What if we loved our neighbors as ourselves?

7. How does this compare to the doctrine of the survival of the fittest?

8. What are the two primary reasons men like the idea of evolution even when they don't actually believe it's true? What are they and what motivates them?

9. What are some of the real reasons people reject Jesus?

10. What are the applications and implications of Matt. 10:32-33?

Chapter Five

Aren't All Religions
Basically the Same?

How can Christians say that Jesus is the only way to reach God? Does this mean other religions are wrong?

There are five major religions in the world. In order of size they are: Christianity, Islam, Hinduism, Buddhism, and Judaism. Fortunately, for those who are willing to take the time and the effort to honestly study the facts, comparing them will allow the truth to emerge.

Each of these religions is mutually exclusive. That is, they each claim to be true, and yet the one thing they have in common is the fact they have almost nothing in common. They disagree on just about every major doctrine of faith. That would include, but not be limited to, the natures of God, man, Jesus Christ; heaven and hell, sin and salvation, etc. Fortunately, each religion has its own so-called "holy book," and each book can be compared and tested.

In logic, the law of non-contradiction states that two antithetical positions cannot both be true in the same sense at the same time. Philip Johnson explains it this way: "…nothing that is true can be self-contradictory or inconsistent with any other truth. All logic depends on this simple principle. Rational thought and meaningful discourse demand it. To deny it is to deny all truth in one fell swoop."

This is good news for critical thinkers and those who are engaged in the search for spiritual truth. Since the major world religions disagree on the major tenets of faith then, logically, either all of them are wrong or one of them is right and the others are wrong. You can be wrong about a lot of things, but if you are wrong about what God says concerning sin and salvation, you will be wrong forever! The following are examples of the blatant contradictions that distinguish Christianity from all other religions. This is some of the most important information you could ever know!

Christianity And Islam

The Koran, the Vedas and the Bhagavad-Gita all contradict the moral laws found in the Bible. See for yourself in the following examples: The Bible teaches that Jesus not only died on the cross, but was resurrected from the dead three days later. This story was supposedly written by *eyewitnesses* of the account. *Six hundred years later*, Mohammed (representing Islam) said that Jesus ascended into heaven without dying at all! The atoning death and the resurrection of Jesus Christ is the core of the Christian faith. If you take Christ's death and resurrection out of Christianity, according to Christian theology, there would be no basis for the forgiveness of sin and no way to get to heaven!

Another excellent example is the Bible's teaching of monogamy in marriage. Genesis says that a man shall leave his father and mother and cleave unto his wife. Ideally, one man is to marry one woman until they are separated by death. By contrast, the Koran teaches that a man can have four wives and as many concubines as he can afford to keep! Nature itself shows that the doctrine of polygamy cannot be divinely inspired since the ratio of men to women has always been 50/50. If men had four wives and numerous concubines there would be a serious shortage of women in the world. This behavior is also *grossly unfair* to women!

Another obvious contradiction when comparing Christianity with Islam is the sixth commandment: "Thou shalt not murder." In Sura 9:5 (and many other places), the Koran *commands* the faithful Muslim to murder or dismember anyone who refuses to convert to Islam. As you can see, the moral law of God reveals that these two religious systems are diametrically opposed to each other. Logically, either they are both wrong, or one of them is right and the other one is wrong.

Christianity & Hinduism

The doctrine of reincarnation is another example of mutual exclusivity. Hinduism teaches that if a man does not achieve moral perfection in this life, he is reincarnated. That means he comes back to life again in a lower form. He could come back as a rattlesnake, a rat, a roach, a buzzard, a cow, or even an insect! That is why many Hindus would starve rather than eat the cows that walk freely through the streets. They believe those cows are their former friends and relatives!

Follow this one through to its logical conclusion and there is another and more immediate problem. If the Hindu took a good look under a microscope at the water they were about to drink, they would see dozens of their friends and relatives having a pool party! Armed with this knowledge, death by dehydration would only be a matter of days away! The fruit of this religious system and the nations that have embraced it is a matter of record. Literally millions of people have lived in abject poverty of body, soul, and spirit for thousands of years and millions more continue to live that way today under this system.

One so-called expert on reincarnation claims that the cycle of life and death could occur as many as 800,000 times before the person is free from suffering and achieves perfect peace (how they would know that, we are not told). Conversely, in Hebrews 9:27, the Bible emphatically states, "It is appointed unto a man once to die and then the judgment." Logically, the ideas of 'one life' and reincarnation could both be wrong, but they cannot both be right. As you can see, all religions are *not* the same.

Christianity & Buddhism

The founder of Buddhism was Siddhartha Gautama. He was born in India around 560 B.C. Buddhism actually evolved out of Hinduism. When Siddhartha found no peace in the so-called sacred writings of Hinduism known as the Vedas and the Upanishads, he sought a better way. He was strongly opposed to the caste system but did accept the Hindu teachings of reincarnation and karma (although not all sects of Buddhism believe in reincarnation). It was while he was sitting under a tree for 40 days that he claims to have experienced *nirvana* (the final state). It was then that Siddhartha became known as the "Buddha" or "the enlightened one."

Buddha did not believe in a personal God. Consequently, Buddhism does not involve worshipping the Creator. Buddhism can be hard to define. Some sects of Buddhism are atheistic, while others are pantheistic. Buddha himself was an atheist, he believed in four noble truths and an eightfold path that would lead to *Nirvana*:

The first is that life is composed of physical and mental suffering. The second is that we suffer because we are attached to the things of the world. The more we want the more we suffer. It is only as we detach ourselves from the cycle of wanting and craving, that we deliver ourselves from suffering. The third is that true happiness is possible on earth, depending upon the degree to which we can detach ourselves from wanting worldly things. If we give up "wanting," we can attain Nirvana. The fourth is that the noble eightfold path is the path toward achieving this detachment and thus attaining perfect peace. In this system there is no god, no eternal life in heaven, only the need to empty ourselves of wanting anything. This supposedly is the path to peace. Clearly Buddhism cannot be reconciled with the Bible. In Matthew 6:33 Jesus said, "Seek first the kingdom of God and His righteousness and all these things will be added unto you."

The Law Of Karma

The law of karma is taught in both Buddhism and Hinduism. Karma is said to be the "law of moral causation." Functioning in this system, you would never help a suffering person because you would interfere with his or her karma. Assisting that person would only prolong their suffering. This is completely antithetical to the teachings of Jesus. Matthew chapter 25 is the climax of Matthew's Gospel. In this scene, time is no more. All mankind is being judged and there are only two classes of people, the sheep and the goats. The sheep are commended for helping those who were suffering and the goats are condemned for their refusal to help the poor. Here again we see a major discrepancy between the major religions of the world. The Bible places a major emphasis on helping the poor, and the law of karma teaches just the opposite. Either they are both wrong (maybe you should only help the rich get richer), or one of them is right and the other is wrong.

Christianity And Judaism

Christianity teaches that Jesus Christ is the fulfillment of the Old Testament prophecies and *is* the Messiah, the Savior of the world. Judaism teaches that Jesus is *not* the Messiah. Logically, either both of them are wrong (there is no Messiah) or one of them is right and the other is wrong.

Here is another major problem for all leaders from every religion in the world who say Jesus was a great moral teacher. Jesus said He was God! Jesus' claim of divinity provides another excellent example of mutual exclusivity. Ask any leader from any of the major world religions and they will freely admit that Jesus was a great moral teacher and a prophet. Unfortunately for them, doing so exposes their ignorance of the problem. Jesus claimed He was God, and sometimes He even used words to say it. The New Testament narratives have Jesus doing things only God could do. That leaves us with only three choices, as C.S. Lewis pointed out:

"A man who was merely a man and said the sort of things Jesus said would not be a great moral teacher. He would either be a lunatic on a level with the man who says he is a poached egg-or else he would be the Devil of Hell. You must make your choice. Either this man was, and is, the Son of God: or else a mad man or something worse. You can shut Him up for a fool, you can spit at Him and kill Him as a demon; or you can fall at His feet and call Him Lord and God. But let us not come up with any patronizing nonsense about His being a great human teacher. He has not left that open to us. He did not intend to."

Therefore, if Jesus was right, the other religions are wrong, and if Jesus was wrong, the other religions are still wrong because they say Jesus was right! As one author (who wishes to remain anonymous) said,

> Buddha said, "I am a teacher in search of truth." But Jesus said, "I Am the truth."

> Confucius said, "I never claimed to be holy." But Jesus said, "Which one of you convicts Me of sin?"

> Speaking of the afterlife, Mohammed said, "I do not know what Allah will do to me." But Jesus said, "I Am the resurrection and the life. He who believes in Me, though he die, yet shall he live."

None of these other men ever claimed to be God. They all said, "God is this way; go this way." But Jesus said, "I am the way, the truth and the life. No man comes to the Father but by Me."

Are all religions the same? The answer is emphatically, "No, they are not." Truth is not a matter of opinion but a matter of fact!

A Closing Illustration

"I was speaking in Santa Barbara, California once, and the professor of Eastern religions, who was an American gentleman, came to argue with me. He asked me if I would speak the next night on why I am not a Hindu. I declined, saying if you throw mud at others, not only do your hands get dirty, but you also lose a lot of ground.

"But he said, 'I dare you to do it, and I'll bring my whole class in philosophy at the end of your talk, to tear you to shreds.' I said, 'that's not a very welcoming thought. But let me do this: I will speak on why I am a Christian, and implicit in that is why I am not a Hindu. And you can bring your philosophy class to talk to me.' Which he did.

"I proposed the fact that Hinduism is loaded with contradictions. I won't go into those details. But at the end of which, he came up to the front and just about wanted to hit me. He said, 'Mr. Zacharias, the reason you portrayed Hinduism the way you did, is because you don't understand the Eastern mind.'

"I couldn't believe it, but I decided to be nice. I said, 'Look sir, there's no point in us getting into a verbal slugfest here, but let me suggest something to you. Why don't you and I have lunch together tomorrow and we'll discuss it? You pay, and I'll pray, and we'll talk about it.'

"So he brought the professor of psychology along with him. He said, 'Ravi, there are two kinds of logic,' (actually, he's wrong: there are more.) 'One is the either/or logic. If you make a statement that is true, the opposite of it is false. It is called the Law of Non-Contradiction. The same question at the same time, meaning the same thing, cannot elicit two opposite answers. If you ask my wife, 'are you expecting a child?' and at the same time if she says yes, and I say no, what will you say?'

"You'll probably say, that's the wrong question, they have a weird sense of humor, she's not his wife, or she hasn't talked to him. You wouldn't walk away saying 'thank you.'" Why not? Because the same question at the same time, meaning the same thing, cannot elicit two opposite answers. That's the either/or logic—the Law of Non-Contradiction—you cannot contradict yourself.'

"He said, 'Ravi that is Western.'" I said, 'Scratch out that line.' He said, 'No, I won't.' I said, 'You're going to have to; you may as well scratch it out now.' He said, 'No, I won't.'" I said, 'Keep going.'

"He said, 'The other kind of logic is Both/And. Not either this OR that: both this AND that. If you ask one Hindu if God is personal, and he says "yes", and you ask another Hindu if God is personal, and he says "no", you ask a third Hindu which of these is right, and he says "both of them", he is very much in keeping with his way of looking at "Both/And". Both personal AND non-personal—that is the Eastern way of thinking.'

"I said, 'Scratch out that line.' He said, 'No, I won't.' I said, 'You're going to have to.' He said, 'No, I won't.' I said, 'Keep going.'

"So finally he established: Either/Or Logic, the Law of Non-Contradiction, is *Western*. Both/And logic, the Law of Dialectic, is *Eastern*. Karl Marx used it: take the employer and the employee, put them together, you get the classless society. Nobody ever shows you one, but at in theory they talk about it. So there it is: Either/Or logic is Western, and Both/And logic is Eastern.

"I said, 'Sir, have you finished?' He said, 'Yes.' I said, 'What you are telling me is this: when I am studying Hinduism, I either use the Both/And system, or nothing else. Is that right?'

Do you know what he said? He put his knife and fork down and he said, 'The Either/Or does seem to emerge, doesn't it?'

"You see, he was using Either/Or logic to prove the Both/And logic. And the more he tried to clobber the Law of Non-Contradiction, the more it clobbered him. The psychologist said, "I think, John, this discussion is over; let's go back.'

"So what I say to you, Ladies and Gentlemen, is this: Jesus' claim was reasonable. The question is, *was he right?* Jesus' claim was reasonable. All religions are exclusive. I looked at that professor and said, 'Sir, I've got some shocking news for you: Even in India, you look before crossing the street. It is either the bus, or you, not both of you.'"

—Ravi Zacharias

A Final Thought

You can be wrong about a lot of things, but if you are wrong about how God forgives sin, you are wrong enough to spend eternity in hell. Many people live like they are never going to die. The fact is life is short, eternity is long, sin is deadly, hell is real and Jesus saves!

Small Group Questions

1. What do we mean when we say the major religions are mutually exclusive?

2. Why can't all religions be right?

3. According to C.S. Lewis, since Jesus claimed to be God, that claim leaves us only three choices concerning Jesus. What are they?

4. What is the first law of logic?

5. How does knowing the first law of logic help to explain how all religions cannot be equally valid?

6. Name two mutually exclusive moral issues that differentiate Christianity from Islam.

7. Name two mutually exclusive points that differentiate Christianity from Hinduism and Buddhism.

8. What character traits separated the sheep from the goats in Matthew 25?

9. What would happen if you took Christ out of Christianity? Why? How does that distinguish Christianity from other religions?

10. The Bible teaches that we are saved by grace alone, through faith alone, through Christ alone—plus nothing! Our good works are the result of our salvation, never the cause of it. How does this distinguish Christianity from all other religions?

Chapter Six

If God Is Merciful, How Can He Punish People in Hell Forever?

I recently saw a huge billboard along a major expressway that read, "Enjoy life now; there is no afterlife." It was sponsored by *The Foundation for Freedom from Religion*. My first thought was, how could they possibly *know* that? On what authority can they make such a claim? The only way you could *know* for a fact whether or not there is life after death would be to die and then come back from the dead to tell us!

There is only one person in history who not only claimed He had the power to come back from the dead, but 2,000 years later, almost 2 billion people actually believe He did! The historical Jesus had such a profound impact on the world by what He said and by what He did, that the world marks time before His birth and after His death. At the time of this writing, it's 2011 "A.D". That is Latin for Anno Domini which means "In the year of the Lord".

The reason we mark time by the birth and death of Jesus Christ is because three days after He was crucified He raised Himself from the dead! Unlike *The Foundation for Freedom from Religion*, Jesus speaks with authority when He speaks of the after-life. He said there is a real place called heaven and a real place called hell.

I believe the doctrine of hell is the most difficult concept that has ever been presented to the mind of man. How can God be merciful and allow people to suffer in hell forever? To many, this appears to be an insurmountable contradiction for Christianity. Nevertheless, the Bible has dozens of references to hell. Having a finite mind and a limited understanding of the mysteries of God, I admit that hell does seem unfair, but by the same token, heaven seems equally unfair. Here are some things you may never have considered about hell.

The Bible Says, It Is Not God's Will For Any Man To Go To Hell

The Apostles and the Prophets affirm the greatness of God's grace conferred on all mankind again and again in the Scriptures. For examples:

John 3:16-17 proclaims that: "For God so loved the world that He gave His only begotten Son, that whoever believes in Him should not perish, but have eternal life. For God did not send the Son into the world to judge the world, but that the world should be saved through Him."

Ezek. 33:11 says, "Say to them, 'As I live!' declares the Lord GOD, 'I take no pleasure in the death of the wicked, but rather that the wicked turn from his way and live.'"

Matthew 25:41 tells us that hell was not made for man but for the devil and his angels.

2 Peter 3:9 says: "The Lord is not willing that any should perish, but that all should come to repentance."

1 Timothy 2:3-4: "This is good and acceptable in the sight of God our Savior, who desires all men to be saved and to come to the knowledge of the truth."

John 1:29: "The next day he saw Jesus coming to him, and said, "Behold, the Lamb of God who takes away the sin of the world!"

There are dozens more of these verses that make it abundantly clear that God would rather have people repent and believe the Gospel.

God Did Not Reject Us; We Rejected Him!

C.S. Lewis put it this way: "Sin is man saying to God throughout his life, 'Go away and leave me alone.' Hell is simply God saying to man, 'You may have your wish.'"

Here is what the Bible says:

Isaiah 30:15: "For thus the Lord GOD, the Holy One of Israel, has said, 'In repentance and rest you shall be saved; in quietness and trust is your strength.' But you were not willing."

Matthew 10:32-33: "Everyone therefore who shall confess Me before men, I will also confess him before My Father who is in heaven. But whoever shall deny Me before men, I will also deny him before My Father who is in heaven."

Matthew 23:37: "O Jerusalem, Jerusalem, who kills the prophets and stones those who are sent to her! How often I wanted to gather your children together, the way a hen gathers her chicks under her wings, and you were unwilling."

Romans 2:4-6 says: "Or do you think lightly of the riches of His kindness and forbearance and patience, not knowing that the kindness of God leads you to repentance? But because of your stubbornness and unrepentant heart you are storing up wrath for yourself in the day of wrath and revelation of the righteous judgment of God, who will render to every man according to his deeds."

It was our sins that nailed Christ to the cross, but it wasn't the nails that held Him there; it was His love for you and me! To reject so great a salvation is to condemn *yourself*.

We Murdered The Son Of God

I'm not so amazed that Jesus raised Himself from the dead. I'm more amazed that He could have died in the first place! Death is the result of sin. That is why all men die, no matter how they die. But Jesus was sinless. How could He have died? The answer is found in 2 Corinthians 5:21, "He made Him who knew no sin {to be} sin on our behalf, that we might become the righteousness of God in Him."

The horrible truth that many people want to avoid is that no one is innocent of the blood of Jesus. The Bible clearly states, "For all have sinned and fall short of the glory of God" (Romans 3:23). The Bible also says, "He (Jesus) was pierced for our transgressions, he was crushed for our iniquities; the punishment that brought us peace was upon him, and by his wounds we are healed. We all, like sheep, have gone astray, each of us has turned to his own way; and the LORD has laid on him the iniquity of us all" (Isaiah 53:5-6, NIV).

In Acts 3, after being filled with the Holy Spirit, Peter preached a sermon and 3,000 people were saved! Three times in that sermon, Peter told his listeners that they murdered the Son of God! This is also what Peter preached in Acts chapters 3, 4, and 5, as well as in 1 Peter 2:24.

In our fallen world and in a corrupt legal system, it's one thing to murder a skid-row bum; it is another thing altogether to murder the President of the United States. If you murder a 'nobody' it is possible, if you have enough money and a 'good' lawyer, to 'beat the rap' on a technicality. But, if you murder the President of the United States, you can be sure that the United States government will bring all of its legal and political power against you in order to insure that you receive the maximum penalty allowed by law. In this case, it was sin, yours, mine, and ours that made it necessary for Jesus to die on the cross. Those who refuse to seek God's forgiveness show no remorse for what they have done.

If you die without Christ as your Savior, when you stand before the Great White Throne of God you will be charged with murdering the Son of God and the penalty is death. Simply stated, because you killed God's Son and show no repentance or remorse, God is going to kill you! That is the point of Luke 20:9-16.

To Preserve Freedom And Defeat Evil

"The fact that humans used God-given free choice to disobey God did not take God by surprise. C. S. Lewis suggested that God, in His omniscience saw that from a world of free creatures, even though they fell, He could work out '. . . a deeper happiness and a fuller splendor than any world of automata would admit.' Or, as Geisler has put it so well, the theist does not have to claim that our present world is the best of all possible worlds, but it is the best way to the best possible world:

"If God is to both preserve freedom and defeat evil, then this is the best way to do it. Freedom is preserved in that each person makes his own free choice to determine his destiny.

Evil is overcome in that, once those who reject God are separated from the others, the decisions of all are made permanent.

"Those who choose God will be confirmed in it, and sin will cease. Those who reject God are in eternal quarantine and cannot upset the perfect world that has come about. The ultimate goal of a perfect world with free creatures will have been achieved, but the way to get there requires that those who abuse their freedom be cast out.

"A critically important factor involved in the suggestion that this may not be the best possible world, but it is the best way to the best possible world, is that God is not finished yet. Too often people fall into the trap of thinking that because God hasn't dealt with evil yet, He is not dealing with it at all. Walter Martin used to say, 'I've read the last chapter in the book, and we win!' Evil will one day be done away with. Just because evil is not destroyed right now does not mean it never will be.

"In view of the above facts, the existence of evil in the world is seen to be compatible with the existence of an all-good and all-powerful God. We can summarize the facts this way:

- If God is all-good, He will defeat evil.
- If God is all-powerful, He can defeat evil.
- Evil is not yet defeated.
- Therefore, God can and will one day defeat evil.

"One day in the future, Christ will return, strip away power from the wicked, and hold all men and women accountable for the things they did during their time on earth (see Matthew 25:31-46; Revelation 20:11-15), and justice will ultimately prevail. Those who enter eternity without having trusted in Jesus Christ for salvation will understand just how effectively God has dealt with the problem of evil." [1]

God Has The Responsibility To Punish Evil

As Creator of the universe, God has the responsibility to punish evil. He has provided the way of escape by our believing, trusting, and relying upon Jesus for salvation, but many refuse His gift and reject His Son.

God created the universe from nothing. But God created man in His own image and likeness, therefore, He expects man to seek Him with all of his heart. As His Word says, "From him to whom much is given, much will be required."

God gave man everything he needed to make an intelligent decision about God and eternity. He wrote the moral law on every man's heart and gave him a conscience. Man has the ability to discern good from evil. Hebrews 4:13 says we are accountable to God for our moral choices.

God is not like us. He is perfect. As high as the heavens are above the earth, His ways are above our ways. God dwells in unapproachable light. He is light and there is no darkness in Him. Nothing impure or unclean can stand in His presence. He is perfectly holy. If God did not punish the unrepentant sinner, He Himself would be unjust. If God, were to overlook even one transgression, He would deny Himself. That He cannot do.

High Treason Is Punishable By Death

Even in man's world, high treason in a time of war has always been punishable by death. For man to exalt his own will above the will of God is an attempt to usurp the throne of God. That is how the archangel Lucifer became the arch-enemy of God and why his name was changed to Satan. The first sin in the universe occurred when Lucifer decided (of his own free will) to say, "I will exalt myself above the throne of God." Lucifer's sin was the pride of covetousness, which is idolatry, an abomination to God. All sin is unbelief. When a person lives his or her life as if God does not exist, God calls it willful rebellion.

God Gave Man A Free Will

Genesis tells us that, "God made man in His image and in His likeness." You are not, never have been, and never will be a robot. God created you as a free-thinking moral agent. You were also designed with a built-in conscience. This means you have the capacity to discern good from evil and to say, 'I should', or, 'I should not.'"

God is sovereign, and in His sovereignty He created man with a free will. How else could our love for God be genuine? This illustration may help connect the dots. Imagine you are playing chess against the world champion chess player. In this case, it would not matter how you move the pieces, he is so much better at the game that you are that he would use *your* moves to win the game! The same principle applies with the sovereignty of God and the free will of man. In the game of life, it does not matter how you move the pieces, it does not matter how Satan moves the pieces; you can move them any way you want to, and God will use those moves to accomplish His sovereign will without ever violating yours! He's that good.

God Is Perfectly Fair And Just

The Bible teaches that there will be different levels of punishment in hell, and different levels of reward in heaven. This is what Jesus is referring to in Luke 12:47-48: "And that slave who knew his master's will and did not get ready or act in accord with his will, shall receive many lashes, but the one who did not know {it,} and committed deeds worthy of a flogging, will receive but few. And from everyone who has been given much shall much be required; and to whom they entrusted much, of him they will ask all the more."

"Hell will be a place of fair treatment. Before anyone goes there, he will stand at a final judgment to determine the exact degree of punishment he will receive. God will be perfectly fair."

"The final judgment is depicted graphically in Revelation 20:11-15. This is the great white throne judgment. The Judge is none other than Jesus Christ (John 5:24-30). All the unsaved receive new bodies and will stand to be judged. Then the books containing the life record of every person and the one special book of life will be opened. The opening of these books shows that those who rejected God's gift of salvation will receive perfect justice.

"In Romans 2:1-16, Paul pointed out that God will look at what people have done with their privileges and opportunities, and that He will be completely impartial and fair (vv.5-1

1). Those who possessed His Word, the law of verses 12-14, will be held accountable for their response to it. Those who never received special revelation will be held accountable only for what they knew (vv. 14-16)."

"No judge or jury fully understands the person on trial. No human being can evaluate the exact degree of accountability in himself or anyone else. We are all profoundly influenced by hereditary and environmental factors beyond our control. Yet we make choices after weighing options. Therefore, we are all accountable-at least to some degree. And God understands to what extent. He also knows how much we need His mercy."

"When the young man who died in a gang war stands before Jesus Christ, he will find that the Lord understands all the circumstances of his short, violent, and troubled life his absent father, his immoral Mother, his disadvantaged peers, his complete ignorance of the gospel message, and his despair. The Lord Jesus will take all these factors into consideration. He knows exactly the degree of responsibility of this young man and will give him a sentence that perfectly suits his offense."

"The rich, respectable landlord who died without Christ may receive a far more severe sentence than most of his tenants, even those who had many brushes with the law. The Lord Jesus will take into account their respective privileges. He will see perfectly the underlying greed, selfishness, and pride of this man. He will understand the sense of despair that was a factor in some of the wrongs done by the tenants. All will receive fair treatment. God, the holy moral Governor of the universe, will dispense perfect justice to all wrongdoers."

"The awesome picture of final judgment in Revelation 20:11-15 led Thomas Carlyle to exclaim: "What a magnificent conception is that of a final judgment! A righting of all the wrongs of the ages." The Lord Jesus Christ will take into account every circumstance, overlooking nothing. He will be the Supreme Court of the universe. No one will be able to appeal His decisions. In fact, no one will feel the need to do so. Every person will acknowledge Him as Lord and admit that His verdict has been absolutely fair and right. It is at this time that everyone will recognize Him to be all He claimed to be, fulfilling the words of Philippians 2:9-11."

Therefore God also has highly exalted Him and given Him the name which is above every name, that at the name of Jesus every knee should bow, of those in heaven, and of those on earth, and of those under the earth, and that every tongue should confess that Jesus Christ is Lord, to the glory of God the Father.[3]

It's Not *Why* But *Who?*

When Job questioned God's fairness in allowing him to suffer "unjustly", God essentially told Job, "You're asking the wrong question. It's not *why* but W*ho?*" God's point was that Job would not be able to comprehend the dynamics of why and how God does what He does. For as high as the heavens are above the earth, so His ways are above our ways! As for those who would still question God's justice, I believe God may want to make the same point to you He made to Job:

Job 38:4 "Where were you when I laid the foundations of the earth? Tell Me, if you have understanding."

Job 38:6 "Whereupon are the foundations thereof fastened? Or who laid the corner stone thereof; when the morning stars sang together, and all the sons of God shouted for joy?"

Job 38:12 "Hast thou commanded the morning since thy days; and caused the day spring to know his place?"

Job 38:17 "Have the gates of death been opened unto thee? Or hast thou seen the doors of the shadow of death?"

Job 38:18 "Hast thou perceived the breadth of the earth? Declare if thou knowest it all."

Job 38:19 "Where is the way where light dwelleth? And as for darkness, where is the place thereof?"

Job 38:22, 23 "Hast thou entered into the treasures of the snow? Or hast thou seen the treasures of the hail which I have reserved against the time of trouble, against the day of battle and war?"

God answered Job's question "Why?" with "Who!" Who are you, O man (with a mind darkened by sin) to question the Eternal Self-Existent One, the Supreme authority Who has jurisdiction over all creation, the One Who dwells in unapproachable light, whom no man has seen or can see and live?

God is saying that a mortal man cannot even begin to comprehend the mind or the holiness of God. Does the clay say to the potter, "Why did you make me like this?" God is God and we are not.

The Eternal Consequences Of Sin

When King David committed adultery with Bathsheba he also arranged to have her husband murdered. In his prayer of repentance, David prayed an insightful prayer: "Against you, you only, have I sinned and done what is evil in your sight..." (Psalm 51:4). What about Bathsheba and Uriah, weren't they sinned against too? This verse reveals that sin is first and foremost against God. Jesus said, "Whatever you do to the least of these My brethren, you do to Me" (Matthew 25:40). God is an infinitely holy and eternal Being (Psalm 90:2). Those who refuse to bow to Him in brokenness and contrition, those who refuse to seek His forgiveness in this life, never receive it.

Why Hell Is Eternal

"Hell must be eternal, because what matters most to man is his present condition. Let me illustrate: suppose you live in a frigid area of the world and you had heat for the last 10 years. But suppose this year catastrophe struck and left you without any heat in the dead of winter, freezing and shivering. Will the fact that you *had* heat for the last 10 years make you happy while you freeze *this* winter? No. What matters most is that you don't have heat this winter. It's true to say that what matters most to you is your present condition. Likewise, suppose that you lived without heat for the last 10 years, but you finally got it this year. Will the fact that you lived without heat for the last 10 years make you unhappy while you sit comfortably and warm now? No. The thing that matters most is your present condition. The same truth applies to all of the pleasure or pain we experience now.

"We must note that *no* temporal pleasures bring true and lasting happiness. Man was created for God and can only be satisfied in Him.

This principle also holds true when we consider the following issues as well.

"What matters most to the unspiritual man is his present physical condition. For example, those who enjoy great fame, or great wealth, or great success, or great beauty, are not troubled by the fact that they did not possess this 10 or 20 years ago. What matters most to them is that they are great, or famous, or successful or wealthy, or beautiful—now!

"Therefore, if the pains of hell end at some point, then at that point man is free from punishment. He would suffer no pain at all and since his present condition is all that matters to him, the *end result* for that man would be that he would not suffer punishment at all.

"Thus it is true to say that a punishment that is not eternal is *in the end* actually not real punishment at all. For if it ends at any point, then, the final condition of that man is that he is free from suffering. All he knows and cares about then is that he is free from punishment.

"But as Deuteronomy 32:35 says, 'Vengeance is Mine and I will repay them in due time.'" Such a punishment can be real only if the end result equals punishment not a state of non-punishment. The only way that the punishment can have an end result which equals punishment rather than non-punishment, is by an ongoing present condition of unhappiness. That is why hell must be and is eternal." [2]

A Closing Illustration

"The alligator saw the boy, but the boy didn't see the alligator. Big, silent, menacing, the alligator with only his eyes and nostrils protruding above the water; looked more like a piece of debris floating in the water, than a dangerous reptile. When it got about fifteen feet away from the boy, it submerged; disappeared from sight. Seconds later it was on the boy, on one of his legs, jaws firmly latched on to one of the boy's legs."

"Before he could even cry for help, the boy was pulled under. That's what alligators do, they drag their prey under water until their victim drowns, and then they eat. Desperately, the boy fought to free himself; until suddenly, surprisingly, he was free. For some unknown reason the alligator had let him go. Frantically, he made it to the surface.

Immediately he started crying out for help. Sure that the alligator would be on him again any second, the boy swam as best he could towards the shore, unable to use his badly injured and bleeding leg very well."

"He made it to shore, he pulled himself up out of the water, on hands and one knee he started to crawl towards his house leaving a trail of blood behind him. He didn't get very far before the alligator was on him again, this time grabbing his other leg, his good leg. The gator had followed him right up out of the water, grabbed him yet again, and was now trying to drag him back into the water. Again the boy screamed, 'Mama, help me!'"

"This time his mother heard him and out the back door she came flying. Once she saw the alligator, she screamed, but she didn't stop. Straight at the beast she ran, grabbing the first thing she saw, a clay flower pot, she threw it at the gator's head. Only for a second did the gator let go of her son, to take one errant snap at her. Then it grabbed her son again!"

"Knowing that if the alligator got her son in the water, it was over, she ran around and grabbed her son by the arms, and pulled with all her strength in the direction away from the water. Alligator pulling in one direction; she in another. Stubbornly she was able to thwart the gator's progress back towards the water. How long they were like that, she didn't know. At times the boy was literally suspended in air as both the alligator and the mother pulled in opposite directions. Then suddenly the alligator let go and disappeared back into the water. She had won; she had won the life and death tug of war for her son."

"Within minutes an ambulance was on the scene, Along with his mother, the boy was taken to a nearby hospital. His recovery took weeks. In time he regained full use of his legs. First day back in school, some of his classmates asked him if they could see the scars on his legs, where the alligator had bitten him. Knowing they wouldn't take no for an answer, he rolled up his pants leg and showed them. But then he added something, 'Never mind those, take a look at these.'" Quickly he rolled up his shirt sleeve, exposing ten puncture wound scars, five on each forearm."

"'How'd you get those?'" his friends wanted to know. 'Did the gator bite your arms, too?' 'No, I got those from my mother. In order to keep the alligator from pulling me into the water, she grabbed hold of me as strongly as she could, digging her nails into my arm in the process. If not for these scars, I wouldn't be here today.'"

A Final Thought

That story reminds me of the world, the flesh and the devil trying to pull you away from the Father, the Son and the Holy Spirit, which would end in your destruction. God wants to save you and Satan wants to kill you. As for those who still question God's justice? Psalm 90:11 says,

> "Who understands the power of Thine anger, and Thy fury, according to the fear that is due Thee?"

What mortal can stand before the Eternal Self-existent One, an eternal being who has the power to speak the universe into existence and question His justice? Especially in light of the fact that He revealed His glory in all of creation, but people still chose to worship themselves instead of the God who made them.

In order for a person to actually go to hell, they will have to live their entire life denying God's existence. In so doing, they exalt themselves above the throne of God. God calls it "idolatry." Every unrepentant sin ever committed every unkind thought, word and deed trampled the blood of Christ and mocked every thing holy. And still, they will have to step over the body of Christ to get there. One of the worst things about being in hell will be the knowledge that they did not have to go there!

End Notes

1. Ravi Zacharias and Norman Geisler, *Who Made God?* 37, 38

2. Adapted and revised from Peter Diamond's essay on hell.

3. Taken from *What Does The Bible Say About Hell?* By Herb Vander Lugt, Copyright 2002 by RBC Ministries, Grand Rapids, MI. Reprinted by permission.

Small Group Questions

1. What consolation do we derive from Point 9 in this chapter?

2. Why must God punish sin?

3. What would be true of God if He did not punish sin?

4. What point are people missing who think God is letting evil prevail?

5. Paraphrase Point 4, about why hell lasts forever.

6. Paraphrase some of the points from the answer to Question 2 above.

7. If according to 2 Peter 3:9, it is not God's will that any should perish, why then do some people perish?

8. What was God's point to us, conveyed through Job?

9. How do you reconcile the sovereignty of God with the free will of man?

Chapter Seven

If God Is God and God Is Good, Why Is There Evil?

When people ask questions like, "If God is good, why is there so much evil?" this begs the question, "How would you know something is evil unless there is a perfect standard of goodness to measure it against?" How can anyone (such as an atheist) call anything good or evil on the basis of a worldview where truth and morality is relative? As C.S. Lewis put it, "A man does not call a line crooked unless he has some idea of a straight line." [1] Only the Biblical worldview can account for the reality of good and evil.

If you really want to know why our world is like it is, you must understand what goes on behind the scenes—in the spiritual realm. A cosmic struggle has been raging between the forces of darkness and the Prince of Peace for untold thousands of years. The battle is for the souls of men. The source of this information is found only in one place: the ancient book we call the Bible!

Our quest begins not with Adam and Eve in the Garden of Eden, but with the angels in Heaven. In Ezek. 28:12-17, God reveals the mystery of iniquity and allows us to see exactly what happened before man was created:

> "Thus says the Lord, 'You had the seal of perfection, full of wisdom and perfect in beauty. You were in Eden, the garden of God; every precious stone adorned you: Your settings and mountings were made of gold; on the day you were created they were prepared. You were anointed as a guardian cherub, for so I ordained you. You were on the holy mount of God; you walked among the fiery stones. You were blameless in

your ways from the day you were created, until unrighteousness was found in you. By the abundance of your trade you were internally filled with violence, and you sinned; therefore I have cast you as profane from the mountain of God. And I have destroyed you, O covering cherub, from the midst of the stones of fire. Your heart was lifted up because of your beauty; you corrupted your wisdom by reason of your splendor."'

When God created the angels, He created one who was "full of wisdom and perfect in beauty." He was known as the "anointed cherub"; his name was Lucifer. I have personally never seen an angel. But according to the Bible, they are *not* Caucasian females with long blonde hair, nor are they little babies with wings floating on clouds playing little golden harps.

According to the Bible, angels are extremely powerful supernatural creatures capable of performing feats of strength far beyond the ability of any mortal man. For example, in 2 Kings Chapter 19, we read the account of one angel that slew 185,000 men from the Assyrian army in one night! And in the Garden of Gethsemane, Jesus said He could have called 12 legions of angels to help Him (Matt. 26:53), which would have been enough sword power to destroy the entire Roman army in one day.

If an angel suddenly appeared in your church next Sunday, no one would remain sitting nonchalantly with their heads in the air. Everybody would hit the floor face down and be scared to death!

For more information on what happened with Lucifer, we turn to the prophet Isaiah, who wrote 750 years before the first advent of Christ. In Isaiah 14:12-14 we read:

"How you have fallen from heaven, O star of the morning, son of the dawn! You have been cut down to the earth, you who have weakened the nations! But you said in your heart, "I will ascend to heaven; I will raise my throne above the stars of God, and I will sit on the mount of assembly in the recesses of the north. I will ascend above the heights of the clouds; I will make myself like the Most High."

There you have it: the first sin in the universe was the pride of covetousness. Lucifer became discontented as the guardian cherub, "full of wisdom and perfect in beauty"; he wanted to be worshipped! It was then that his name was changed from Lucifer (which means 'light-bringing') to Satan (which means 'adversary').

The Rebellion In Heaven

Based on Revelation 12:4, it is believed that one third of the angels followed Lucifer in his attempt to exalt himself above the throne of God. So, here we have a third of the angels in opposition against God. The question was, what should God have done about it? He could have vaporized them instantaneously. He could have crushed the rebellion with a word! The problem with that approach is obvious: if the Creator had simply wiped out the fallen angels, the worship in Heaven would have been tainted by fear. In 1 John 4:18-19 God's Word says,

> "There is no fear in love; but perfect love casts out fear, because fear involves punishment, and the one who fears is not perfected in love."

Even though God is sovereign, one thing He cannot do is force someone to love Him; forced love is a contradiction in terms. If God were to violate your free will on this point, true love would not be possible. So, God said in effect, "I will prove my love, not with a show of force, but with a demonstration of perfect love." That is where we come in. We are "Exhibit A" to all the host of Heaven that God is love. John 3:16, the central theme of the Bible, sums this up for us: "For God so loved the world that He gave His only begotten Son, that whoever believes in Him should not perish, but have eternal life."

The Garden Of Eden

A close look at what happened in the Garden of Eden is most revealing. God created a small planet and set up a test for all to see. Man was placed in a perfect environment. Adam and Eve were created with a conscience, a free will, and without sin. Genesis 2 tells how the Lord God gave them everything they needed to live in abundance. He provided Adam with a beautiful helpmate and told them to "Be fruitful and multiply." He said, "From any tree of the garden you may eat freely." As He was about to leave them alone for their honeymoon (my paraphrased version), He turned around and said, "Oh, by the way, there is one thing: just don't eat from the tree of the knowledge of good and evil, for in the day that you eat from it you shall surely die. Have a great day."

When the Lord forbade them from eating fruit from the tree of the knowledge of good and evil, they were now put in the position where good was not the only thing they could do. There was now one prohibition. In order for man to be morally tested, a choice to obey or disobey was presented. All the angels in Heaven are watching God's plan of redemption unfold in real time. So, what happened? Genesis 3 says: "They both took from its fruit and ate; then the eyes of both of them were opened, and they knew that they were naked." They chose to disobey God and, as a result, the curse of sin infected man and the Earth.

God Must Let Sin Run Its Course

God gave man free will not just so our love could be genuine, but because He wants all to see what happens when the creature exalts himself above the Creator. Why? So it will never happen again.

The staggering truth is that even the angels, who have spent their entire existence in the presence of God, are amazed that men love the Lord even though they have never seen Him. Luke 15:10 says: "In the same way, I tell you, there is joy in the presence of the angels of God over one sinner who repents."

In John 20:25-29, Jesus promised a special blessing to those who have believed and not yet seen the Lord,

> So the other disciples told him, "We have seen the Lord!" But he said to them, "Unless I see the nail marks in his hands and put my finger where the nails were, and put my hand into his side, I will not believe it." A week later his disciples were in the house again, and Thomas was with them. Though the doors were locked, Jesus came and stood among them and said, "Peace be with you!" Then he said to Thomas, "Put your finger here; see my hands. Reach out your hand and put it into my side. Stop doubting and believe." Thomas said to him, "My Lord and my God!" Then Jesus told him, "Because you have seen me, you have believed; blessed are those who have not seen and yet have believed." (NIV)

Jesus Christ is God's chosen instrument to prove to all of creation that His love is perfect. But didn't God know that all this would happen beforehand? The answer is, yes, of course! God had a plan to overcome all the effects of sin. Jesus was "the Lamb of God slain from (*before*) the foundation of the world." This is not 'Plan B'. This is how God is preparing the perfect world in eternity. When all is said and done, there will never be another rebellion in heaven, because no one will ever doubt God's love or His righteous rule of the universe ever again. And the saints of God will live happily forever after!

A Closing Illustration

A Barber's Story: Why Does God Allow Suffering?

"A man went to a barber shop to have his hair and his beard cut, as always. He started to have a good conversation with the barber who attended him. They talked about so many things and various subjects. Suddenly, they touched the subject of God.

"The barber said: 'Look, man, I don't believe that God exists as you say.'"

"'Why do you say that?' asked the client."

"'Well, it's so easy, you just have to go out in the street to realize that God does not exist. Oh, tell me, if God existed, would there be so many sick people? Would there be abandoned children? If God existed, there would be no suffering nor pain. I can't think of loving a God who permits all of these things.'"

"The client stopped for a moment, thinking, but he didn't want to respond as to cause an argument. The barber finished his job and the client went out of the shop. Just after he left the barber shop he saw a man in the street with long hair and a beard (it seems that it had been a long time since he had his hair cut and he looked so untidy). Then the client again entered the barber shop and he said to the barber, 'You know what? Barbers do not exist.'"

"How can you say they don't exist?" asked the barber.

"Well I am here and I am a barber."

"No!" the client exclaimed. "They don't exist because if they did, there would be no people with long hair and a beard like that man who walks in the street."

"Ah, barbers do exist, what happens is that people do not come to me."

"Exactly!"—affirmed the client. "That's the point. God does exist, what happens is, people don't go to Him and do not look for Him. That's why there's so much pain and suffering in the world."

A Final Thought

Why Does God Remain Silent?

Imagine a young man driving up to an unmanned toll booth at 3:00 a.m. The toll is 40 cents and all he has are two quarters. He is thinking about pulling away without paying just as he sees a police car pull up right behind him. Will he put in the money? Of course! The test comes when he thinks no one is looking. The quality of a man's faith is what he does when he *thinks* he is alone. God is testing us. Hebrews 4:13 explains it: "And there is no creature hidden from His sight, but all things are open and laid bare to the eyes of Him with whom we must give account."

Can you imagine how God feels when His people praise Him in church, and pray to Him in the secret closet of prayer (i.e., when no one is looking)? Revelation 5:8 says: "And when He had taken the book, the four living creatures and the twenty-four elders fell down before the Lamb, having each one a harp, and golden bowls full of incense, which are the prayers of the saints." The point is, our prayer and praise is precious to God!

End Notes

C.S. Lewis, *Mere Christianity* (New York: Macmillan, 1952), p. 45.

Small Group Questions

1. Why wouldn't God just destroy the angels when they rebelled?

2. Why is God going to allow sin to run its course?

3. Why has God remained silent?

4. What did Lucifer do that caused him to become Satan? What is the lesson for us?

5. What is God telling us in Hebrews 4:13?

6. Why is God testing us?

7. What do we learn from the story of Job and how does it apply to us?

8. In Revelation 5:8 we discover that God keeps the prayers of the saints in bowls. What is God trying to tell us there?

9. How has God demonstrated His love for us?

10. What is God's reason for allowing evil in the world?

Chapter Eight

What About Those
Who Have Never Heard?

Many people have never heard of Jesus or even seen a Bible. How can they be held accountable? That is similar to the question, "Where did God come from?" The fact is, there is no one who has never heard. Here is why: going all the way back to Genesis 4:26, the Word of God says, "And men began to call upon the name of the Lord." That was before the Bible was written, before there were any synagogues or churches, before radio, TV, CDs, DVDs and, as far as we know, there were no teachers or preachers of any kind! How can that be? We start in the book of Psalms 19:1-3 where we read:

> "The heavens declare the glory of God; the skies proclaim the work of his hands. Day after day they pour forth speech; night after night they display knowledge. There is no speech or language where their voice is not heard."

The truth is, God has revealed Himself in nature (Romans 1:18-21) and in conscience (Romans 2:12-16). So all an honest, thinking person has to do is take a good inside their own heart, then look at the sun, the moon, the stars, and consider the wonders of creation to *know* that anything so perfectly designed and well balanced as is our world and universe, could in no way have made itself. There is no excuse for unbelief.

Example: The Human Body

Human beings are "Exhibit A" of the great power and wisdom of God. He made us in His image and in His likeness. Psalms 139:14 tells us that we are "fearfully and wonderfully made."

The human body is for all practical purposes infinitely more complex and efficient than anything built or even conceived by man. You name it: a Cray super-computer, the Space Shuttle, an atomic reactor. These systems are simple and inefficient when compared to the human body.

An adult body consists of 100 trillion cells, 206 bones, 600-plus muscles, and 22 internal organs. Every square inch of the human body is covered by about 19 million skin cells. Approximately 1 billion cells are replaced every hour as your DNA transmits coded information to new cells; your body completely regenerates itself every 7 years!

The human brain is made up of 12 trillion cells. Each cell connects to 10,000 other cells, making 120 trillion connections—more than all the telephone systems in the world combined. The brain sends and receives information to and from the cells through the nervous system instantaneously. By contrast, the fastest supercomputer in the world costs $100,000,000, is as large as a 6,000 square foot house, and still cannot produce one original thought!

The human eye has more than 137,000,000 light-sensitive cells, which translate everything you see instantaneously through your nervous system and your brain *sees*! Your eyes can communicate your emotions and are said to be the windows of your soul. Scientists estimate that the muscles in your eyes make more than 100,000 movements a day.

Your blood circulates through 60,000 miles of arteries, veins, and capillaries (enough to go around the world almost three times), and completes the cycle 1,000 times a day! The human heart beats more than 2.5 billion times in an average lifetime.

About 10,000 taste buds on the surface of your tongue and on the roof of your mouth make eating enjoyable. The digestive system then breaks down the food into smaller molecules, and extracts the nutrients which are then absorbed into the blood. The blood delivers the nutrients to the cells throughout the body, which enables the release of energy for muscular movement.

The muscular system is made of more than 600 muscles divided into two groups—voluntary and involuntary. Voluntary muscles work only when you tell them to, for example, when you play the piano, swing a bat, or you close your eyes and bend over to smell the aroma of a freshly baked loaf of bread. Involuntary movements would include your heartbeat, the blinking of your eyes, and the movement of your diaphragm so you breathe without even thinking about it!

More than 30 facial muscles cause your face to reflect how you feel and what you're thinking. Muscles cause you to smile, to frown, to create looks of surprise, happiness, sadness, confusion, anger, joy, wonder, and every other emotion you can think of.

The cardiovascular system, the respiratory and circulatory systems, the nervous system, the skeletal and muscular systems, the reproductive system, the digestive system, the immune system, and the five senses are marvels of wisdom and ingenuity far beyond the ability of mindless evolution to design and build. As for energy efficiency, the whole system runs on bread and water!

The Heavens Declare His Glory

In case you have not read chapter one yet, the next couple of paragraphs are worth repeating. The earth revolves at a constant speed of 1,000 miles an hour at the equator. Incredibly, as passengers on Starship Earth, we are at this moment flying through time and space (orbiting the sun) at a comfortable cruising speed of 67,000 miles an hour! We make the 584,000,000 mile journey once every 365.25 days and our "on time" arrival record is better than any train or airline in the world!

The Milky Way galaxy is 100,000 light years across and 10,000 light years in diameter at the center. To get from one end of the galaxy to the other, you would have to travel at the speed of light (186,282 miles every second) for 100,000 years! The earth is 26,000 light years from the center of the galaxy. If you were to take a commercial airliner from earth to the center of our own Milky Way galaxy, traveling at 550 miles an hour, it would take you 278 quadrillion years to get there!

Not only do all the planets in our solar system revolve around the sun, but the entire Milky Way galaxy (consisting of hundreds of billion of stars), revolves once every 250 million years! From our position in space, we are flying around the center of the galaxy at a traveling velocity of 550,000 miles an hour! What causes all the stars to stay in place as we circle the galaxy like a giant merry-go-round? What powers it? Who steers it? Why don't the stars collide? How could this happen all by itself? What about the hundreds of billions of other galaxies in the universe, who is directing all this traffic? Where did it all come from?

Because of the regularity of the physical laws that govern our universe, astronomers can chart the position of stars, planets, moons, and asteroids far into the future with accuracy and precision. Here is what Albert Einstein said about natural law in his book *The World As I See It*:

> "The harmony of natural law reveals an intelligence of such superiority that, compared with it, all the systematic thinking of human beings is an utterly insignificant reflection.

> ". . . it seems to me, (this) is the attitude of even the most intelligent human being toward God. We see a universe marvelously arranged and obeying certain laws, but only dimly understand these laws. Our limited minds cannot grasp the mysterious force that moves the constellations."

What About Handicapped People?

Obviously, a blind person cannot see the beauty and the majesty of God's creation. Also, people handicapped in other ways could not appreciate God's creation as well as other people. But in Ecclesiastes 3:11, King Solomon said: "...He has also set eternity in their heart." And in Romans 2:14-16 we read:

> "For when Gentiles who do not have the Law do instinctively the things of the Law, these, not having the Law, are a law to themselves, in that they show the work of the Law written in their hearts, their conscience bearing witness, and their thoughts alternately accusing or else defending them, on the day when, according to my gospel, God will judge the secrets of men through Christ Jesus."

Here God tells us that everyone is morally accountable for how we live. Romans 2:15 refers to the moral law of the Ten Commandments. The fact is, whether people will admit it or not, every man knows in his heart it is wrong to murder, to commit adultery, to steal and lie. God put a moral compass called conscience in the heart of every man. The same idea is found in Romans 1:18-20:

> "For the wrath of God is revealed from heaven against all ungodliness and unrighteousness of men, who suppress the

truth in unrighteousness, because that which is known about God is evident within them; for God made it evident to them. For since the creation of the world His invisible attributes, His eternal power and divine nature, have been clearly seen, being understood through what has been made, so that they are without excuse."

Let me illustrate. The Mona Lisa is one of the most famous paintings in the world. The painting itself is proof positive that there was a Leonardo DaVinci. While none of us alive today have ever actually seen him we can see what he left behind. Can you imagine having a debate on a college campus as to whether or not the Mona Lisa was the result of a great master or if it was the result of blind chance and time? What person in his or her right mind would want to take the position that the Mona Lisa painted itself?

How much more does God expect us to ponder the wonders of creation and give Him the glory He deserves! In Psalms 14:1, the Bible says, "Only the fool says in his heart there is no God." But Deuteronomy 4:29 says,

> "But if from there you seek the LORD your God, you will find him if you look for him with all your heart and with all your soul."

I have often referred to this verse as God's address. This verse teaches a very important principle—everyone who truly seeks after God with all of their heart will find Him, for God will make Himself known!

A Closing Illustration

This is the true story about a minister who was driving through northern Iran with his wife. They came to a small village where he decided to buy water. As he stops his car, he notices a man leaning against the wall of the shop with a beard and a machine gun. The wife sees the man's gun and face, takes a Bible in Farsi, and puts it in her husband's pocket. She says, "Give that man a Bible."

Her husband looks at the beard, looks at the gun, and says, "No."

She says, "No, no, no, seriously, give it to him. Give him the Bible."

So he says, "I'll pray about it." He goes into the shop, comes out with bottles of water, and they drive away.

The wife looks at her husband. "You didn't give him the Bible, did you?"

He said, "No, I prayed about it. It wasn't the right thing to do."

She said, "You should have given him one."

He disagrees and they go back and forth. So the wife bows her head and prays out loud fervently that her husband might listen to God. At that point, they have a friendly discussion that married couples have from time to time that ends with the words, "Fine! If you want me to die, I will.'"

The husband turns the car around and goes back into the village. He gets out of the car, walks up to the man, and places a Bible in his hands. The man opens it and starts to cry.

He said, "I don't live here. I live three days walk from here. But three days ago an angel came and appeared to me and told me to walk to this village and wait until someone had given me the Book of Life. Thank you for giving me this book."

A Final Thought

It is common knowledge (at least by those of us who follow these things) that many people, especially in the Middle East, are having dreams and claiming to see visions of Jesus! God speaks to us in many and various ways. He speaks through Creation; He speaks through the Bible, He speaks through the Holy Spirit, and He can speak through His people. He has spoken through angels; through circumstances, preacher and teachers, Gospel tracts, books and maybe even this one. He can speak through a donkey if He wants to.

He spoke to me a long time ago while I was on my knees crying out to Him. He flooded my soul with His love and I have never been the same. God is not an impersonal force; He is not an obscure power. God is a person. He has a mind, a will and emotions. He loves goodness and He hates sin. God's Word is an invitation to get to know Him. Get a Bible and start reading it prayerfully, seek the Lord with all your heart and don't stop until you find Him. You haven't found anything worth living for until you find something worth dying for. He died for you because he loves you that much.

Small Group Questions

1. What is the answer to the question, "What about those who have never heard?" Explain why this is true.

2. What does the Mona Lisa have in common with Psalms 19:1-3?

3. What does 1 Corinthians 2:9 mean?

4. Paraphrase Romans 1:18-20.

5. What does the complexity and efficiency of the human body tell us about God?

6. Genesis tells us that man is made in the image of God. What attributes does man have in common with God?

7. Look up Matthew 18:3. What characteristics do children have that Jesus wants to see in us, and in our relationship to Him as our heavenly father?

8. What characteristics do we inherit as children that we are to outgrow as we mature in Christ?

9. What is God saying in Deuteronomy 4:29?

10. What are the implications of Revelation 3:20?

Chapter Nine

Why Doesn't God Answer My Prayers?

Washington D.C. is where the political power game is played on a scale that most of us cannot even begin to comprehend. In Washington, it's not what you know but who you know that counts. The ultimate power in the universe of Washington is access to the Oval Office and the President of the United States.

As Christians we have something infinitely greater than the Oval Office. We have direct access to the Throne of God, and no appointment is necessary. Prayer is the great privilege of the Christian and a great responsibility. Unfortunately, precious few of us realize it. We fail to take advantage of the incredible opportunity to spend time with the Supreme Commander, who has jurisdiction over everything in the universe!

Why does so much prayer seem to go unanswered? And why do we have to pray at all since God knows everything? The problem is not with God but with our understanding, or lack thereof concerning prayer. Let me begin by saying that talking to God is one of the most normal, natural, sane, rational, intelligent things a person can do. Studying the Word of God, prayer and giving are the three greatest tests of true spirituality.

There are many types of prayer, and the Bible provides ample proof of the efficacy of prayer. There are prayers of intersession and supplication, prayers of thanksgiving, prayers of praise, prayers of confession, prayers of dedication, etc. But in its most basic form, prayer is simply talking to God. It should be as natural as breathing.

We do well to remember that God is a person. How would you like it if every time someone spoke to you, all they ever did was ask for favors? Not even a "Hello," or, "How are you?" How long would a relationship like that last? God is not an impersonal force, He is our friend! In order to have a friend, one must show thyself friendly. Usually, it's best to get to know someone before you start asking for favors. How do you get to "know" God? You cultivate the relationship by reading His book. The better you know the Word of God the better you know the God of the Word. Then you pray.

According to Herbert Lockyer's excellent book entitled, *All the Prayers of the Bible*, "… the Bible records no fewer than 650 definite prayers, of which no less than 450 have recorded answers."

God Always Answers Prayer. It's Either, Yes, No, or Wait! Sometimes God Says, "Yes." There Are Several Reasons:

It Is The Will Of God

I John 5:14 is crystal clear,

> "And this is the confidence which we have before Him, that, if we ask anything according to His will, He hears us."

The Bible does not contradict itself. If what you believe about prayer does not agree with every other verse in the Bible, your understanding of that verse is not completely correct. I John 5:14 is absolute. In John 15:5-7, Jesus speaks of abiding in Him,

> "I am the vine, you are the branches; he who abides in Me, and I in him, he bears much fruit; for apart from Me you can do nothing. "If anyone does not abide in Me, he is thrown away as a branch, and dries up; and they gather them, and cast them into the fire, and they are burned. "If you abide in Me, and My words abide in you, ask whatever you wish, and it shall be done for you."

What does it mean to "abide" in Christ? When Jesus said, "I am the vine, you are the branches," that verse is saying, "You draw your life from Christ!" There is no life apart from Him and the one who abides in Him produces fruit. Those who produce no fruit cannot expect to appropriate the promises of answered prayer and according to verse 6, those branches will be cut off.

Verse 7 is not an unconditional guarantee that if you have enough faith and get all the sin out of your life, that God will give you *whatever you want*. He is far too wise for that. We can ask for and get anything we want when what we want is in line with what He wants. Why would anyone who abides in Christ want anything other than what He would want?

The Sacrifice Of Humility

In Psalms 51:16-17, we discover that real prayer is more than mere words. To approach a holy God you need the right heart attitude.

> "For Thou dost not delight in sacrifice, otherwise I would give it; Thou art not pleased with burnt offering. The sacrifices of God are a broken spirit; a broken and a contrite heart, O God, Thou wilt not despise."

Long before David penned the words to Psalm 51, Genesis 18:27 revealed how Abraham approached God—in great humility,

> "And Abraham answered and said, 'Now behold, I have ventured to speak to the Lord, although I am {but} dust and ashes.'"

As you read through the rest of the story in Genesis, Abraham called upon God again and again for wisdom, guidance and strength. Abraham prayed, and in humility, he trusted the Lord to provide for his every need and God supplied it.

When The Answer Brings Glory And Honor To Him

The Bible provides us with numerous examples of people who prayed and received answers. But they are not like the prayers we hear today. When you hear most people pray they all sound very similar, like a short prepared speech. And they always end, "In Jesus' name, amen."

Have you ever given God a reason why you think He should answer your prayers? Imagine for a moment that your boss is very wealthy, very generous, and also happens to be your closest personal friend. If you needed a favor from him, would you talk to him the same way most Christians talk to God when you hear them pray? Do you ever pray to God and talk to Him like you would to a close friend? And is there a Biblical precedent for such an idea?

As you look at the Old Testament prophets, in many cases when they had a request, they accompanied their requests with the reasons *why* God should answer them.

Genesis 18 records the story of Sodom and Gomorrah. God tells Abraham that a cry of distress has risen up to heaven, because the sin in Sodom is great. God plans to destroy the city and Abraham appeals to God and His sense of justice. Here is the exchange from Genesis 18:24-32. Abraham says to God,

> "Suppose there are fifty righteous within the city; wilt Thou indeed sweep {it} away and not spare the place for the sake of the fifty righteous who are in it? Far be it from Thee to do such a thing, to slay the righteous with the wicked, so that the righteous and the wicked are {treated} alike. Far be it from Thee! Shall not the Judge of all the earth deal justly?"

Here we have Abraham reminding God that He is just and fair. He says in essence, "You couldn't possibly destroy the righteous along with the wicked!" So God responds,

> "If I find in Sodom fifty righteous within the city, then I will spare the whole place on their account." And Abraham answered and said, "Now behold, I have ventured to speak to the Lord, although I am {but} dust and ashes. Suppose the fifty righteous are lacking five, wilt Thou destroy the whole city because of five?" And He said, "I will not destroy {it} if I find forty-five there." And he spoke to Him yet again and said, "Suppose forty are found there?" And He said, "I will not do {it} on account of the forty."
>
> Then he said, "Oh may the Lord not be angry, and I shall speak; suppose thirty are found there?" And He said, "I will not do {it} if I find thirty there."
>
> And he said, "Now behold, I have ventured to speak to the Lord; suppose twenty are found there?" And He said, "I will not destroy {it} on account of the twenty." Then he said, "Oh may the Lord not be angry, and I shall speak only this once; suppose ten are found there?" And He said, "I will not destroy {it} on account of the ten."

Can you believe this? Abraham is actually haggling with God! He is giving Him reasons, good reasons why answering this prayer is in God's best interest.

Moses provides another example in the book of Exodus. Incredibly, after all the miracles the Israelites experienced in the Exodus from Egypt, and at Mt. Sinai, they turned to idolatry and worshipped a golden calf. God was understandably angry and was about to bring judgment when Moses interceded for them. Here is the exchange from Exodus 32:7-14,

> Then the LORD spoke to Moses, "Go down at once, for your people, whom you brought up from the land of Egypt, have corrupted {themselves.} They have quickly turned aside from the way which I commanded them. They have made for themselves a molten calf, and have worshiped it, and have sacrificed to it, and said, 'This is your god, O Israel, who brought you up from the land of Egypt!'" And the LORD said to Moses, "I have seen this people, and behold, they are an obstinate people. Now then let Me alone, that My anger may burn against them, and that I may destroy them; and I will make of you a great nation." Then Moses entreated the LORD his God, and said, "O LORD, why doth Thine anger burn against Thy people whom Thou hast brought out from the land of Egypt with great power and with a mighty hand? Why should the Egyptians speak, saying, 'With evil {intent} He brought them out to kill them in the mountains and to destroy them from the face of the earth'? Turn from Thy burning anger and change Thy mind about {doing} harm to Thy people. Remember Abraham, Isaac, and Israel, Thy servants to whom Thou didst swear by Thyself, and didst say to them, 'I will multiply your descendants as the stars of the heavens, and all this land of which I have spoken I will give to your descendants, and they shall inherit {it} forever.'" So the LORD changed His mind about the harm which He said He would do to His people."

Moses, quoting from God's Word is reminding God of His own promises of mercy and grace. Then he appeals to God concerning His reputation (What will the Egyptians say?) and God grants his request!

Moses provides God with the reasons why He should spare the people and God *changes His mind*!

Our next lesson comes from Numbers 14:11-21. The context of this story is the failure of the Israelites to believe God concerning the Promised Land. The Lord said He would go before them so they could take the land from the Canaanites who were exceedingly wicked. Unfortunately, they feared the people and rebelled against God. This was a blatant form of idolatry—something God hates!

> And the LORD said to Moses, "How long will this people spurn Me? And how long will they not believe in Me, despite all the signs which I have performed in their midst? "I will smite them with pestilence and dispossess them, and I will make you into a nation greater and mightier than they."

Moses appeals to God and gives Him the reasons why He should spare His people from judgment,

> But Moses said to the LORD, "Then the Egyptians will hear of it, for by Thy strength Thou didst bring up this people from their midst, and they will tell {it} to the inhabitants of this land. They have heard that Thou, O LORD, art in the midst of this people, for Thou, O LORD, art seen eye to eye, while Thy cloud stands over them; and Thou dost go before them in a pillar of cloud by day and in a pillar of fire by night. "Now if Thou dost slay this people as one man, then the nations who have heard of Thy fame will say, 'Because the LORD could not bring this people into the land which He promised them by oath, therefore He slaughtered them in the wilderness.' "But now, I pray, let the power of the Lord be great, just as Thou hast declared, 'The LORD is slow to anger and abundant in lovingkindness, forgiving iniquity and transgression; but He will by no means clear {the guilty,} visiting the iniquity of the fathers on the children to the third and the fourth {generations.} "Pardon, I pray, the iniquity of this people according to the greatness of Thy lovingkindness, just as Thou also hast forgiven this people, from Egypt even until now." So the LORD said, "I have pardoned {them} according to your word; but indeed, as I live, all the earth will be filled with the glory of the LORD."

Does God Actually Change His Mind?

God is not whimsical. He *always knows* what He is going to do. This verse is speaking anthropomorphically. An example would be, "The sun sets in the west." The sun does not actually "set" it only appears to do so. We are speaking anthropomorphically. In the same sense, God does not "change His mind" in the sense that we change our minds. God is omniscient. He knows every thing there is and everything that could be. Let me illustrate.

If I choose to ignore God and live in sin, God's Word has already declared, He will reject me on judgment day. But *if I repent*, God has already promised to save me. It's not that God is just one minute, and merciful the next. He is always both. It's my heart that has changed, not His.

Why, if God knows everything, do I need to pray? In many cases what God wants to see is, "How important is this to you?" The fervency of your prayer shows how much *you* care! In Ezekiel 22:30-31 we discover an amazing truth,

> "And I searched for a man among them who should build up the wall and stand in the gap before Me for the land, that I should not destroy it; but I found no one. Thus I have poured out My indignation on them; I have consumed them with the fire of My wrath; their way I have brought upon their heads, declares the Lord GOD."

This is an incredible verse. God was looking for someone to pray and ask Him to spare the nation from judgment, but He found no one. The obvious implication is that He was willing to show mercy, but since none of them even cared enough to intercede for their own nation, He "brought their own way upon them!" Either way, God's will would be done.

There is often, but not always a direct correlation between how much we care about a just cause and how much God is willing to help. If *we* don't care enough about our nation to cry out to God, why should He save it?

Consistency Counts

In Matthew 18:1-4, Jesus calls a child to Himself and says to the disciples,

> "At that time the disciples came to Jesus, saying, 'Who then is greatest in the kingdom of heaven?' And He called a child to Himself and set him before them, and said, 'Truly I say to you, unless you are converted and become like children, you shall not enter the kingdom of heaven. Whoever then humbles himself as this child, he is the greatest in the kingdom of heaven.'"

Notice, Jesus did *not* say "become childish." He said, "Unless you become *like* a child." One of the many wonderful attributes we see in children is persistence, especially when it comes to asking for something they want. They are experts in the art of sales and negotiating, and under normal circumstances, they don't take "no" very easily.

I have raised 5 children. I never had to train them to be persistent or of the benefits of asking again and again. It's natural to them. If the answer is "No" or "Wait," the immediate response is "*Why?*" If I say "No" again, they will provide me with all the reasons why I should say "Yes." If they still don't get what they want, the next step is to form a think—tank in order to pool their ideas and develop a new strategy. Then they decide which child has the best chance of closing the sale. This approach can be very effective. They know I love them and want to say "Yes" as often as possible. So what does all this have to do with prayer?

Everything— Keep Reading!

Luke 11:5-9 says,

> "And He said to them, 'Suppose one of you shall have a friend, and shall go to him at midnight, and say to him, "Friend, lend me three loaves; for a friend of mine has come to me from a journey, and I have nothing to set before him'; and from inside he shall answer and say, "Do not bother me; the door has already been shut and my children and I are in bed; I cannot get up and give you anything.'" "I tell you, even though he will not get up and give him anything because he is his friend,

yet because of his persistence he will get up and give him as much as he needs. And I say to you, ask, and it shall be given to you; seek, and you shall find; knock, and it shall be opened to you."

The lesson here is not that God is a crank and if you bug Him enough He will give you what you want just to get rid of you. The lesson is fervency; to filter out what is not important. Prayer is not like impulse buying or trivial pursuit. God does not show His favor to the curious, He shows His favor to the serious.

Sometimes God Says, "No." There Are Several Reasons:

It Is Not The Will Of God

In Jeremiah 7:16-19 in reference to Judah, God said to Jeremiah,

"So do not pray for this people nor offer any plea or petition for them; do not plead with me, for I will not listen to you. Do you not see what they are doing in the towns of Judah and in the streets of Jerusalem? The children gather wood, the fathers light the fire, and the women knead the dough and make cakes of bread for the Queen of Heaven. They pour out drink offerings to other gods to provoke me to anger. But am I the one they are provoking? declares the LORD. Are they not rather harming themselves, to their own shame?"

And in Luke 22:41-42, Jesus prays,

"And He withdrew from them about a stone's throw, and He knelt down and {began} to pray, saying, 'Father, if Thou art willing, remove this cup from Me; yet not My will, but Thine be done.'"

I remember a TV preacher at the end of the "show" instructing his listeners with, "You don't *ask* God, you don't say; 'If it's your will' you *DEMAND* from God!" He was literally growling and gnashing his teeth in the camera as he said the words, "You *demand* from God!"

Friend, if it is not God's will for you to have something, you can demand all day and then demand all night. You can hold your breath until you turn blue in the face, stomp your feet on the floor, and throw a temper tantrum. You can name it and claim it, but if it is not God's will for you to have what you are asking for, you are *not* going to get it. There is a very good reason for this. Does a loving parent give a child anything and everything they want? God knows so much more than we do, He loves us too much to give us whatever we want. If God gave me everything I asked for I would be spoiled, more proud than I am already, and useful for nothing! Thank God He does *not* answer all our prayers the way we want Him to.

To Achieve A Higher Purpose

Three times the Apostle Paul asked God to remove a thorn in his flesh and three times God said, "No. My grace is sufficient." Paul was being protected from self-exaltation. In the Garden of Gethsemane Jesus asked His Father, "If there is another way, let this cup pass from Me." The answer was, "No." Sometimes God uses suffering to bring about a greater good. The story of Joseph in Genesis 37-50 is a classic example of how God brought triumph out of tragedy.

Suffering can be used to test our faith and our character (Genesis 22:1-2), to purify us in order to bear more fruit (Isaiah 48:10, John 15:1-2), to remove impurities and strengthen us (1 Peter 1:6-7), to chastise or correct us (Hebrews 12:5-7), and to bring us to repentance (Revelation 3:19). God will also give us the strength we need to endure it (1 Corinthians 10:13).

A Sinful Lifestyle

Proverbs 28:9 says,

> "He that turneth away his ear from hearing the law, even his prayer shall be an abomination."

The phrase "turns away his ear" literally means to turn off, or avoid. The Hebrew word for "hearing" is (shaw—mah); it is a primitive root meaning "to hear intelligently with the implication of obedience." Do you reward a willfully disobedient child? Simply stated, if you do not care to listen to God, why would you expect Him to listen to you? Psalms 66:18 says,

> "If I regard iniquity in my heart, the Lord will not hear me."

And Proverbs 15:8 says,

> "The sacrifice of the wicked is an abomination to the LORD: but the prayer of the upright is his delight."

Asking With Wrong Motives

God not only knows *what* we do, He knows *why* we do it! James 4:3-4 says, "You ask and do not receive, because you ask with wrong motives, so that you may spend {it} on your pleasures. You adulteresses, do you not know that friendship with the world is hostility toward God? Therefore whoever wishes to be a friend of the world makes himself an enemy of God."

I remember seeing a TV preacher (I'm not kidding) commanding his congregation to, "Repeat after me. I want my money now!" And they were all standing shouting at God, "I want my money now! I want my money now!" I'm sorry, but I did not watch the rest of the "show." Apparently, they were expecting money to start falling out of the sky. I don't know how else they would have received it, "now!"

Mistreating Other People

1 Peter 3:7 says,

> "You husbands likewise, live with {your wives} in an understanding way, as with a weaker vessel, since she is a woman; and grant her honor as a fellow heir of the grace of life, so that your prayers may not be hindered."

If you are not right with people you are not right with God. In I John 4:20 we read,

> "If someone says, 'I love God,' and hates his brother, he is a liar; for the one who does not love his brother whom he has seen, cannot love God whom he has not seen."

Lack Of Fervency And Character

James 5:16-18 says, "The effective, fervent prayer of a righteous man avails much." Stated negatively, the ineffectual, lackadaisical prayer of an unrighteous man avails nothing!

Sometimes God Says "Wait"

We live in an age of instant gratification. The faster we can get whatever we want, the better. In the "olden days" our parents often saved up the money they needed to make large purchases.

In case you haven't noticed, God is not in a hurry. He promised Abraham he would have a son, and 25 years later He shows up and says in essence, "Okay, it's time." It was 9 months later that 100 year old Abraham and his 90 year old wife, Sarah, had their first child! That is why Isaac is called, "The son of promise."

The Israelites were enslaved for 400 years before God delivered them from Egyptian bondage. Of course it took that long for the tribe of 70 to become a nation of 2-3 million. Nevertheless, our God does things in His time, not ours.

The sacrificial system lasted for 1,500 years providing a literal, historical, and theological context, so when Jesus came along, the idea of the blood sacrifice for the atonement of sin would make sense.

God required approximately 1,500 years to complete the Bible. So far, it covers about 6,000 years of mankind's past and present. We do not know when this age will come to a close. We do know, thankfully, God is very patient.

To Summarize

We see four primary principles of prayer in these passages:

- They wanted God's will, God's glory and God's reputation to be pre- eminent in the answer.
- The person praying was humble before God.
- They were persistent because the cause was worth while.
- While they were not perfect, they had a heart to obey God.

One of the reasons so few of us have a dynamic prayer life is because we are convinced God will do whatever He wants anyway, so why bother? In 1 Corinthians chapter 10, God's Word says the things that happened to the Israelites in the wilderness were written for *our* example and *our* instruction! The point is, they missed the abundant life they could have had because they failed to trust in, believe in and rely upon God.

There are many answers to prayer recorded in the Bible, and many answers to prayer are recorded in the lives of countless people today. You don't have to look far to find them, just ask around. A good place to start would be your local church. The bottom line on prayer is simple. God is sovereign. He has His reasons for sometimes saying "Yes," sometimes saying, "No," and sometimes saying, "Wait." Our job is to trust Him no matter what. He knows what He's doing and He hates complaining.

A Closing Illustration

The Providence Of God And Prayer

It was a warm summer day in St. Louis. I was at a weekend conference with about 3,000 people in attendance. There was a break in the teaching, and I was walking between the stage and the front row to the book tables. I heard my name called and looked in that direction. I saw an old friend I hadn't seen in years. We talked briefly when she introduced me to Lester. We all sat down and Lester asked me where I was from. I said, "Chicago. Where are you from?"

Lester said, "Monterey Mexico!"

In a slightly astonished tone I said, "Monterey, Mexico, what brings you here?"

Lester said, "I'm trying to get into the jail in Chicago."

Now I am beyond astonished; I am totally blown away! I said, "I am a Chaplain at the county jail in Chicago. I can get you in there with no problem!" So after the conference, Lester met me the following week at the jail. Together, we provided a chapel service. I preached a message and Lester prayed for each man individually.

After the service, I introduced Lester to one of the other chaplains. I said, "Lester, this is Rob; Rob, this is Lester."

Lester has a thick accent, so Rob asked Lester, "Where are you from?"

Lester: "Monterey Mexico."

Rob: "I have been trying to get into an orphanage in Monterey to distribute Bibles."

Lester: "That is my ministry. I can get you into all of the orphanages in Monterey!"

The next day, they rode off into the sunset together, driving a truck that was filled with Spanish Bibles! Was that a coincidence or was that the providence of God in answer to prayer?

A Final Thought

I leave you with James 5:17-18,

> "Elijah was a man with a nature like ours, and he prayed earnestly that it might not rain; and it did not rain on the earth for three years and six months. And he prayed again, and the sky poured rain, and the earth produced its fruit."

Small Group Questions

1. What is the most basic kind of prayer?

2. Have you ever experienced God answering prayer? Can you share the details?

3. Have you ever prayed a prayer and, looking back, are glad now that God did *not* answer it? Why?

4. What are some of the different kinds of prayer?

5. What are some of the reasons prayer goes unanswered?

6. Look up John 9:1-3. What are some of the reasons that God does miracles?

7. Look up Ezekiel 22:30-31. What do we learn from this passage?

8. Read Luke 11:5-9. Is the lesson that God is a crank and if you bug Him enough He will give you what you want just to get rid of you? If not, then what is the lesson?

9. Look up 1 Peter 3:7. What is God trying to tell us?

10. What is God trying to tell us in James 5:17-18?

Chapter Ten

I'm a Good Person; Why Do I Need a Savior?

You may be a good person, but by whose standard? If God compared you to Adolph Hitler you would probably compare very favorably. But what if He compared you to Jesus Christ? The Ten Commandments are God's perfect moral standard and by that standard none of us is "good". See for yourself:

First Commandment:
You Shall Have No Other Gods Before Me

Stated positively, that means you *shall* 'Love the LORD your God with all your heart, mind, soul and strength.' So, what does it mean to love God? Jesus said, 'If you love me, you will obey My commands.' But God is perfect! To obey that commandment according to God's standard would require perfect obedience, which is another way of saying sinless perfection. No *mere* man has ever loved God like that! If the greatest commandment is to love God with all your heart, then the greatest sin cannot be murder. The greatest sin must be not to love the God who created you more than the things He created! This brings us to the next commandment.

Second Commandment:
You Shall Not Make For Yourself Any Graven Image

"You are not to make a god with your hands or with your mind. I have people tell me that my god is a god of love; he would never send anyone to hell. I agree with them. Their god never would send anyone to hell, because their god doesn't exist. He's a god made in their own image. The Bible says, 'God is a consuming fire', who has a passion for justice, holiness, righteousness and truth, who will by no means clear the guilty, but will hold every man accountable for every idle word that he speaks.'" [1]

The first commandment tells us who to worship, and the second commandment tells us how to worship—in spirit and in truth. That is, by faith and according to His Word, the Bible.

Third Commandment:
You Shall Not Take The Name Of The Lord Your God In Vain

When a man stubs his toe, or hits his thumb with a hammer, he usually takes the name God or the name Jesus—the name that is above every other name, the name which represents a blessing—and uses it as a curse!

The ancient Jew was so fearful of breaking this command that he dared not even speak the most holy name of God, because the commandment goes on to say, "the LORD will not leave him unpunished who takes His name in vain."

This command is far broader then yelling out the name God or Jesus in anger. This commandment is broken when people who call themselves Christians honor Him with their lips, but live like the world.

Fourth Commandment:
Remember To Keep The Sabbath Holy

When Jesus fulfilled the law (by dying on the cross) the Old Testament ceremonial law of feasting, fasting and the sacrificing of animals was complete. The Sabbath typified the rest that would come when the sinless Lamb of God Jesus Christ would offer Himself as a sacrifice for sin once and for all!

The principle of taking one day out of seven to worship God still applies but in a new and better way. We go to church on Sunday to offer a sacrifice of praise! We celebrate the finished work of Christ and in that rest, acknowledge the God who created us, the God who sustains us, and the God who purchased our salvation with His own blood (Acts 20:28).

Fifth Commandment:
Honor Your Father And Mother

In the Old Testament, to rebel against your parents was punishable by death. When you dishonor your father and mother you dishonor God, because He commanded us to honor our parents, as well as everyone in authority over us. What would happen to our world if everyone humbled themselves and honored those in authority and all who were in authority honored God?

Sixth Commandment:
You Shall Not Murder

Jesus said, "You have heard that it was said, 'You shall not murder . . .' but I say to you that whoever is angry with his brother (or calls him empty headed or a fool) will be in danger of judgment and the fires of hell" (Matthew 5:21, 22). When someone does something wrong to you and you 'decide' not to forgive that person, you have crossed the line into sin. Jesus taught that we are to forgive even as we have been forgiven (Matthew 6:14, 15).

Furthermore, when you choose not to forgive someone, you are judging that person as unworthy of forgiveness, which only God has the right to do. And refusing to forgive someone makes you a hypocrite with arrogance beyond belief, because the very things you refuse to forgive in others (sin), in God's eyes, you are just as guilty of yourself!

Seventh Commandment:
You Shall Not Commit Adultery

Jesus said, "You have heard that it was said, 'You shall not commit adultery.' But I say to you that whoever looks at a woman to lust after her has committed adultery already, in his heart" (Matthew 5:28). This is very serious, because man looks only on the outer appearance, but God looks at a person's heart (1 Samuel 16:7). So God knows all about it!

Eighth Commandment:
You Shall Not Steal

People are not thieves because they steal; they steal because they're thieves. Do you know how much you have to steal to be a thief? *Anything*! It's not the value of the thing; it's the principle of the thing. Jesus said, "Whatever you do to the least of these my brethren you do to Me" (Matthew 25:40). The Bible says that thieves will not inherit the kingdom of God (1 Corinthians 6:9-10).

Ninth Commandment:
You Shall Not Lie

How many lies do you have to tell to be a liar? The answer is, the same number of times Adam and Eve had to eat the forbidden fruit to be found in rebellion against God and worthy of death, just once. God means what He says, and He says what He means. Revelation 21:8 reveals how serious God is about this: "...all liars, their part {will be} in the lake of fire and brimstone which is the second death."

Tenth Commandment:
You Shall Not Covet

Stated positively, this means: "Be content with what you have" (Hebrews 13:5b). That is, be satisfied with what you can make with your own hands and your own mind. You are not supposed to desire what already belongs to your neighbor; including his house, his car, his wife, his title, his position, or his bank account.

Many if not most Americans are in bondage to materialism. The average American home now owes almost $8,000 on their credit cards! We call them "credit cards" but they are actually "covet cards". They allow us to buy things we don't need with money we don't have, to impress people we don't even like. Materialism is a form of idolatry.

The Gospel

In the Old Testament, an animal was offered as a sacrifice for sin. The animal had to be perfect, which was symbolic of moral purity. The animal had to be without spot and without blemish; the spot was inherited, and the blemish was acquired.

When the Virgin Mary was impregnated, by the Spirit of God, what was begotten nine months later was God in a human body. Because Jesus was not born of the seed of man, He had no inherited sin (spot). And, because He lived a perfectly holy life, He had no acquired sin (blemish). That is why the Bible refers to Him as "the Lamb of God" (John 1:29).

When Jesus died on the cross, His death satisfied the righteous penalty of the Law, which was death. God, as the supreme authority over the universe and having jurisdiction over sin and death, can legally declare those who accept Christ's sacrifice on their behalf not only not guilty, but righteous. As a result of Christ's death He can bestow His perfect mercy without compromising His perfect justice!

How Does Christ's Death Apply To You?

While living in the Chicago area, I became engaged to the young lady who is now my wife, Susan. While I believe it was the Lord's will for me to marry Susan, I still wanted the blessing of my future in—laws who lived in Nevada. My fiancée flew out a few weeks before I did. I flew out 2 weeks later and arrived right on time. I knocked on their door, and they invited me in. Later that night we had a wonderful dinner together. A few hours later, I was escorted to my own private bedroom, and was told to, "Make yourself at home." The next day, my future mother in-law said, "You're going to need to get around, so here are the keys to the car."

Can you imagine what might have happened if I had knocked on the wrong door—a perfect stranger—and asked for food, a place to stay for the night, the keys to their car, and their daughter's hand in marriage? A sandwich might have been achievable, but the rest would have been out of the question!

Religion vs. Relationship

I knocked on the right door. In John chapter 10, Jesus said, "I am the door." I came in the right name, in this case it was, "Susan." In Acts 4:12 the Bible says, "There is no other name under heaven given among men whereby we must be saved." The whole context of Acts 4 is about the Lord Jesus Christ! I came to the right door, I came in the right name, and I came with the right motive, which was love. In 1 John 4:19 the Bible says, "We love Him because He first loved us." I was accepted by the parents by virtue of the fact that I had a love relationship with their daughter. Now everything that belonged to her (by inheritance) would now belong to me as well. That is precisely how salvation works with God.

"Therefore having been justified by faith, we have peace with God through our Lord Jesus Christ, through whom also we have obtained our *introduction* by faith into this grace in which we stand; and we exult in hope of the glory of God" (Romans 5:1-2).

Christianity is not a religion, it's a revelation. And once you've had the revelation, it leads you to a personal love relationship with God through His Son the Lord Jesus Christ! When you come to God the Father in the name of His Son, Jesus, you are "accepted in the beloved" (Ephesians 1:6). The Bible refers to true believers as, "the Bride of Christ." And He (Christ) is our Heavenly Bridegroom." We are called 'children of God' now (Phil. 2:15, 1 Jn. 3:1, 2, 10; 5:2), and are members of the family of God! We become "co-heirs with Christ" (Rom. 8:16-17)! So someday, we will share in the heavenly inheritance of Christ Himself!

A Closing Illustration

I received a call one day from an organization known as *Inner City Impact* in Chicago. The man asked me if I would be interested in addressing their youth group at a weekend retreat. I said, "I would love to address your youth group. What would you like me to teach on?"

The answer was, "Sexual purity."

I gulped, and asked what age group they were and the answer was, "High School." My heart sank as I hung up the phone. I remember thinking to myself, *I would much rather be locked up in a maximum security prison and preach on the love of God, rather than face these young people, and try to convince them that purity is the best way to go.* Please don't misunderstand. I believe with all my heart that this is one of the most critical issues of our day, and it needs to be addressed. My problem was, I had never preached on that particular subject to that particular age group before, and I don't like to preach unless I have something compelling to say.

At the retreat, I had approximately 50 girls on my left, and 50 boys on my right. I asked the girls, "How would you like to know the three secrets that will make you the most eligible girl in your entire neighborhood for marriage?"

I was met with a resounding, "Yes!"

I said, "A real man, a good man, will be looking for three things in a wife: First, someone he can respect, second, someone who is special, and third, someone who is a challenge. Now watch and listen very carefully."

I walked over to the boys and said, "Gentleman, if you had the opportunity to marry one of two women, both equally beautiful, both equally talented, both equally gifted, and both of them have dynamic personalities; in fact, they're identical twins. The only difference between the two is, one of them has had multiple sexual partners, and the other one is a virgin. How many will take the virgin? Raise your hands." Without hesitation, *all of them* smiled and raised their hands. I said, "Gentleman, keep your hands right where they are!" I walked back over to the girls and said, "Ladies, I don't care what they're telling you in the back seat of the car on Saturday night, take a good look at 'em now, because there's the naked truth!" I could see many of them turning their heads like curious puppies, obviously thinking to themselves, "Wow! There's a revolutionary concept. I never thought of that before."

I went on to say, "For those of you who are still virgins, just remember that you can always become like the girls who are not, but they can never become like you. As for those who have lost their virginity, I have some good news for you. It's never too late to start living right. The next best thing is 'secondary virginity.' You can decide today to remain celibate. If you have to wait one, two, five, or ten years for the right man to come along, and you tell him you have been waiting for him all that time, I guarantee you he will think you are someone he can respect, you are special, and you are a challenge." They *all* applauded![1]

A Final Thought

A couple of years after this event, I found myself speaking at a church in Chicago. I was unaware of the fact that many of the young people who attended that weekend went to this church. After the service a bunch of girls cornered me and said, "Do you remember us?" Frankly, I had to admit I did not. They said, "We remember you from the weekend at Camp Awana. Do you remember the illustration you gave us about purity?"

Now the lights were on in my mind and I said, "Yes!"

They said, "What you said really stuck with us. All of us have been saving ourselves for our husbands!" I cried then and I'm crying as I write this. James 1:25 and 2:10 calls the moral law "The perfect law of liberty. Holiness is the key to happiness. God's moral law is written on every man's heart. Obedience is key to living the abundant life Jesus speaks of. God has revealed Himself and His plan of redemption to the whole world and it's written in the heart of every man. Read Psalm 119, take two aspirin and call me in the morning. You'll never be the same if you follow the advice in the Word of God.

I leave you with this promise from the Word of God,

> "And those who have insight will shine brightly like the brightness of the expanse of heaven, and those who lead the many to righteousness, like the stars forever and ever."

— Daniel 12:3

Small Group Questions

1. What do the Ten Commandments have to do with sharing the Gospel? (Compare Exodus 20:20 to Romans 3:20; 23; 31; 6:23; 7:7, and Galatians 3:24)

2. What is sin? How does knowing what sin is, help you?

3. Compare Exodus 31:18 with Matthew 5:17 and Romans 7:7. What do you think God is trying to tell us?

4. Now see Romans 2:15. What are the implications of this verse?

5. How do we overcome sin? Look up and discuss the following verses: Psalms 119:11, Matthew 1:21, Mark 10:26-27, 2 Corinthians 10:5, Galatians 5:22, 1 John 2:14, and Revelation 12:11.

6. Where does sin begin and how does it develop? See James 1:14-15.

7. Look up Matthew 5:30. Why can't Jesus be speaking literally in this verse even though what He is saying is literally true?

8. What are the differences between a religion and a personal relationship?

9. How do you cultivate a relationship with God? See Deut. 4:29, Prv. 2:1-5, Matt. 7:7-8, Jas. 4:8, Rev. 3:20.

10. What does God require of you to get saved? See Mark 1:15, Acts 26:20, Rom. 10:9-11, Eph. 2:8-9.

There's No Such Thing as a Good Excuse

People have many excuses for rejecting Christianity, such as too many hypocrites in the church, too many contradictions in the Bible, the Crusades, God's order to kill the Canaanites etc.

We've all heard the expressions, "There's no such thing as a good excuse." And, "He can't see the forest because of the trees." When it comes to Christianity, many people hide behind excuses to cover the real issue, which is either moral or psychological rather than intellectual. Pride plays a major role in people's unwillingness to even talk about God.

Why do you suppose it is that the name of Jesus can clear out a room faster than any other name in the world? Jesus Christ is the light of the world. Light and darkness in Scripture are metaphors for good and evil. Men hate Jesus because just the sound of His name brings conviction of sin. Men hate religion because it forces them to face things they don't want to face. The darkness hates the light because the light exposes the darkness.

Many people believe what they *want to believe* without ever really taking the time to find out if what they believe is true and right! There are people who are afraid to seek God because the first thing on His agenda is to send them off to Africa as missionaries! In cases like this, it's not because people can't believe, it's because they don't want to. That is a matter of the will rather than the intellect. Many of us are psychologically oriented rather than truth-oriented. We live by feelings rather than facts. "Don't confuse me with the facts, just tell me what I want to hear," seems to be the reality for many people. I will never forget asking a waitress, "I'd like to get your opinion on something."

She said, "I'm sorry. I don't think," and she walked away!

Well, that attitude is a common problem in society. Many people honestly do not want to know the truth about what's happening in our world. It's easier to 'hide your head in the sand' to ignore the harsh realities of life. Many are content to spend their free time watching TV or playing games, (this way they don't have to think).

Many people have no interest in seeking alternative news sources, and accept whatever spin the major news networks tell them about current events. People who spend too much time watching TV end up becoming desensitized morally and spiritually. There are powerful forces at work in our world (both seen and unseen) that want to "dumb down" the general public and keep them there. The fact is, the better informed we are, the better off we are. I read one statistic that said the vast majority of college graduates never read another book after graduating! Listen to what Jesus said in Matthew 24:37-39,

> "But as the days of Noah were, so also will the coming of the Son of Man be. For as in the days before the flood, they were eating and drinking, marrying and giving in marriage, until the day that Noah entered the ark, and did not understand until the flood came and took them all away, so also will the coming of the Son of Man be."

In other words, the people became so involved in the affairs of this life they become completely oblivious to the true condition of the world around them—until it was too late. Now, let's examine some of the excuses people give for rejecting Christianity.

Excuse #1: Too Many Hypocrites In Church

The question, "What about all the hypocrites in the church?" is really a lame excuse to cover the real issue. What people fail to realize when they use this excuse is this: anybody can call himself a Christian, but *calling* yourself a Christian does not make you one any more than eating at McDonalds makes you a hamburger! This fact alone should eliminate the judging of Christianity by counterfeit "Christians".

The hypocrites that *are* in the church however, actually serve to vindicate Christianity rather than condemn it. For inquiring minds who want to know how this is possible, here is the answer. In the time of Christ, the biggest hypocrites were known as the Pharisees. While not all Pharisees were hypocrites, Jesus preached against their religious pride and hypocrisy calling it evil. Nearly 30% of the Gospels are dedicated to exposing and denouncing religious hypocrisy. In Matthew chapter 23, Jesus pronounced seven woes on the religious hypocrites of His day.

I'll never forget a weekend seminar I led for a group of prison inmates in Southern Illinois. After the seminar, as I was driving out of the compound, I approached the last check-point and stopped. A female officer approached the car and this is how the conversation went,

"Are you with the church group?" I answered in the affirmative. She said, "Okay, go ahead."

"Can I ask you something?"

"Sure, go ahead."

"Are you a churchgoer?"

"Nah, there's too many hypocrites down there."

My first thought was to say, "Why don't you come join us, we could always use one more?" But I knew that would not win her heart. So, I said, "Let me ask you something. If you discovered you had a counterfeit $20 bill in your pocket, would you throw all the rest of your twenties away?" She replied, "No." "Well," I said, "Remember this. Wherever there is a counterfeit, there also must of necessity be a genuine article. Yes, there are some hypocrites in the church, but in most churches at least 20% of the people are the kind who would literally give you the shirts off their backs. Jesus told us to follow Him, not the hypocrites!"

Jesus Christ Himself warned us again and again, saying, "Watch out for false Christs, false apostles, false prophets, false teachers, false brothers, tares among the wheat, and wolves in sheep's clothing!" The harshest words Jesus ever spoke were directed at the religious hypocrites.

It's also helpful to realize the distinction between hypocrisy and imperfection. A hypocrite is a person who projects a false sense of piety while living a double life. In reality, a true Christian admits he is imperfect and needs forgiveness for his or her sin. That is not hypocrisy; that is honesty and transparency!

The Bible makes a distinction between practicing sin (that is, living a sinful lifestyle) and 'blowing it' once in a while because we are weak. Before I was a Christian, I enjoyed my sin; now I hate it. Before I was saved I made arrangements to sin; today, I run from it. There is a difference between committing an act of sin and being tempted to sin. Now, I repent for even entertaining an impure thought. And as I grow spiritually, with God's help I am better able to control my thought life.

The Christian life is a process of growth. Babies can't eat steak. It takes time to grow teeth. When I first received Christ I had been smoking cigarettes for 20 years. I did not master the addiction overnight. It took three more years before I finally (with God's help) put them down for good. I was not a hypocrite; I hated smoking, but I was weak. Do you see the difference?

"Too many hypocrites in the church" is nothing more than a poor excuse to hide the real reason for rejecting Christianity. This makes the person who uses it a hypocrite himself. Jesus said, "Follow Me." Only He was perfect. The claim of hypocrisy is only a valid excuse to reject Christianity if you can show that Jesus was a hypocrite—and that you cannot do!

Excuse #2: Contradictions In The Bible

When I hear this excuse I like to begin by asking, "Can you show me one?" For those rare individuals who can point out an apparent contradiction, I like to ask them, "If I can explain this to your satisfaction, are you willing to learn more about Jesus? This will reveal the true motives of the skeptic's heart.

What we are doing by asking this question is separating those who are interested in light from those who are only interested in heat. If they say "No", then the real problem is not a supposed contradiction in the Bible, but something else. The real reason for rejecting the Gospel is almost always based on moral rather than intellectual grounds. The real issue is usually rooted in pride.

If they *are* interested in light, you may try to answer their question. In reality, most of the apparent contradictions in the Bible are easily cleared up by looking at the literal, historical, and grammatical context of Scripture.

Here is one of the best examples of an apparent contradiction in the Bible—between Paul and James in Ephesians 2:8-9 and James 2:21. Paul says,

> "For by grace you have been saved through faith; and that not of yourselves, {it is} the gift of God; not as a result of works, that no one should boast."

And James says,

> "Was not Abraham our father justified by works, when he offered up Isaac his son on the altar?"

In Ephesians chapter 2, Paul is saying that a person is saved (that is, from the penalty of sin, and enters heaven) as a result of "faith" and not because of any good works he performed. Salvation is a *gift* from God which was purchased for us when Jesus Christ died on the cross. He paid our sin debt in full, and salvation is available freely to all who trust in Christ. The Bible teaches that we are saved by grace alone, through faith alone, through Christ alone, plus—nothing! Our good works are the *result* of our salvation, *never* the *cause* of it. Here is the verse, in context, that unbelievers say contradicts Eph. 2:8-9. It is found in James 2:15-24:

> "If a brother or sister is without clothing and in need of daily food, and one of you says to them, 'Go in peace, be warmed and be filled', and yet you do not give them what is necessary for {their} body, what use is that? Even so faith, if it has no works, is dead, {being} by itself. But someone may {well} say, "You have faith, and I have works; show me your faith without the works, and I will show you my faith by my works." You believe that God is one. You do well; the demons also believe, and shudder. But are you willing to recognize, you foolish fellow, that faith without works is useless? Was not Abraham our father justified by works, when he offered up Isaac his son on the altar? You see that faith was working with his works, and as a result of the works, faith was perfected; and the Scripture was fulfilled which says, 'And Abra-

ham believed God, and it was reckoned to him as righteousness', and he was called the friend of God. You see that a man is justified by works, and not by faith alone."

The problem that James addresses is common even today. There are many people who give intellectual assent to Christianity; they claim to be "believers", but their lifestyles reflect no change in behavior and they produce no fruit. James is saying, if your faith is genuine, the kind that saves you, everyone will know you have it because it will result in a life of faithfulness.

Paul is talking about the root of our salvation (faith) and James is talking about the fruit of our salvation (good works). Paul refers to the foundation of our faith, and James is talking about the house that is built on that foundation. Paul is referring to what only God can see, and James is talking about what man sees. Jesus said, "Let your light shine before men that they may see your good works and glorify your father in heaven." James is saying, going to church doesn't make you a Christian anymore than eating at McDonald's makes you a hamburger! If there is no change in your life style, there has been no real change in your heart. So, don't be deceived into thinking that intellectual assent is synonymous with heart knowledge. Knowing *about* Jesus and *knowing* Jesus are two different things.

Believing Jesus existed in the past is not the same as having a personal relationship with Him in the present! In the end, it's not what was professed but what was practiced, not according to what was said but what was done. But even what was done was not to earn salvation; the good deeds were done out of love for the One who saved us!

Excuse #3: God Ordered The Killing Of Men, Women, Children, And Animals.

First, as the sovereign LORD of the universe, God has the right (since He is also the Creator, the Sustainer, and the Redeemer of all mankind), to give life and to take it away. Fortunately, He is also just and merciful. It was God who first introduced (and explained the rationale behind) the doctrine of justifiable homicide. The Canaanites were involved in the grossest forms of immorality, which leads to disease. In order to contain and eradicate disease and in order for God to protect the rest of mankind, everyone including the women, the children and the animals had to be destroyed by fire. It's also helpful to know that God gave them 500 years to stop their sinful behavior. I'd say He is actually very patient.

Excuse #4: What About The Crusades?

Some critics of Christianity are quick to point out that the Crusades were carried out by "Christians" but that is not exactly correct. The Crusaders were a military force consisting of Roman Catholics and mercenaries.

The city of Jerusalem had been taken by the Muslims in the 7th century. In 1095 Pope Urban II sanctioned the Crusaders to fight back against Muslim aggression and take back the holy city. Unfortunately, his intention was not so he could give it back to the Jews and Christians, which would have been a just cause for war. He wanted it for the glory of Rome! The Crusaders were promised an indulgence (the false promise of a free ticket to heaven) if they would fight for the Pope.

During the Crusades, not only Muslims, but Jews and Christians were either massacred or sold into slavery. The Crusaders sought to rid Europe of "ecclesiastical heretics." This included anyone who refused to convert to Roman Catholicism. They were robbed, raped, murdered, and burned at the stake. The Crusades ended in 1291. That is *not* how Jesus taught His disciples to fish for men. The Crusaders killed in disobedience to God's commandment not to murder. Jesus told His followers to love their enemies, not to murder them. Christ said if His kingdom were of this world His disciples would fight for Him. Admittedly, the Bible does say, "There is a time for war and a time for peace." However, the Crusaders were taking orders from a corrupt imperial pope, and neither their methods nor their motives were in line with God's "time for war". Jesus did not say, "Follow the Crusaders," He said, "Follow Me."

Excuse #5: Church Is Boring And Irrelevant

Church was never meant to be boring or irrelevant. If your church is boring, saturate the place with your absence and find one where the pastor is interesting and relevant, and where the worship is inspiring. This will also require you to have ears to hear. If your attitude is wrong, the finest Bible teacher and the greatest worship in the world can't help you. In that case, *you* are the problem.

In this context someone has compiled a humorous list called, "*Ten Reasons I Never Wash*." The parallels (excuses) between not washing and not going to church are obvious:

- I was forced to wash as a child.
- People who wash are hypocrites—they think they're cleaner than other people.
- There are so many kinds of soap, I can't decide which is right.
- I used to wash, but it got boring.
- I wash only at Christmas and Easter.
- None of my friends wash.
- I'll start washing when I am older.
- I really don't have time.
- The bathroom isn't warm enough.
- People who make soap are only after *your money*.

When it comes to something as serious as your eternal destiny, don't make excuses. Think through the excuses you are making and then ask, "What if I'm wrong?"

End Notes

For an exhaustive resource on the apparent contradictions in the Bible, I recommend, *When Critics Ask*, by Norman Geisler.

Small Group Questions

1. Can you think of any other excuses people use to reject Jesus and what is the best way to answer them?

2. Look up Ephesians 2:8-9 and James 2:21. How is this not a contradiction?

3. What problem does James 2:21 address?

4. What is the difference between intellectual assent and the 'heart knowledge' of Jesus?

5. Look up John 6:26. Why did Jesus have to say that?

6. What is the difference between genuine hypocrisy and the weakness in all of us?

7. What does the author mean when he distinguishes between those who are interested in 'heat' rather than 'light'? What question can you ask to disarm those who only want to argue?

8. Why do so many people want to hide from Jesus? Check out John 3:19 and Proverbs 29:25.

9. If church is boring, what might the real problem be? Why?

10. Look up John 8:24. What did Jesus mean by this?

Questions for your Atheistic Professor

The True Story Of A Famous Atheist "Coming Out Of The Closet"

"Dr. Richard Lumsden was a cell biologist, molecular biologist, and a superb electron microscopist. He had many published papers in many peer-reviewed journals, and is listed as the 1975 winner of the Henry Baldwin Ward Medal.

"You couldn't claim Dick Lumsden's faith came from the culture in which he lived, like you might with someone from the 1500s. If anything, he was a product of the anti-creationist second half of the twentieth century. Dr. Richard D. Lumsden was fully grounded in Darwinian philosophy and had no reason or desire to consider Christianity. Science was his faith: the facts, and only the facts. But at the apex of his professional career, he had enough integrity to check out the facts, and made a difficult choice to go where the facts led him, against what he had been taught, and against what he himself taught. His life took a dramatic turnaround, from Darwinist to creationist, and from atheist to Christian.

"Dr. Richard Lumsden was professor of parasitology and cell biology at Tulane University. He served as dean of the graduate school and published hundreds of scientific papers. He trained 30 PhDs. Thoroughly versed in biological sciences, both in knowledge and lab technique, including electron microscopy, he won the highest world award for parasitology. All through his career he believed Darwinian evolution was an established principle of science, and he took great glee in ridiculing Christian beliefs. One day, he heard that Louisiana had passed a law requiring equal time for creation with evolution, and he was flabbergasted. How stupid, he thought, and how evil! He used the opportunity to launch into a tirade against creationism in class, and to give them his best eloquence in support of Darwinism. Little did he know he had a formidable opponent in class that day. No, not a silver-tongued orator to engage him in a battle of wits; that would have been too easy. This time it was a gentle, polite, young female student.

"This student went up to him after class and cheerfully exclaimed, "Great lecture, Doc! Say, I wonder if I could make an appointment with you; I have some questions about what you said, and just want to get my facts straight.

Dr. Lumsden, flattered with this student's positive approach, agreed on a time they could meet in his office. On the appointed day, the student thanked him for his time, and started in. She did not argue with anything he had said about evolution in class, but just began asking a series of questions:

"How did life arise?"

"Isn't DNA too complex to form by chance?"

"Why are there gaps in the fossil record between major kinds?"

"What are the missing links between apes and man?"

"She didn't act judgmental or provocative; she just wanted to know. Lumsden, unabashed, gave the standard evolutionary answers to the questions. But something about this interchange began making him very uneasy. He was prepared for a fight, but not for a gentle, honest set of questions. As he listened to himself spouting the typical evolutionary responses, he thought to himself, *this does not make any sense. What I know about biology is contrary to what I'm saying.*

"When the time came to go, the student picked up her books and smiled, "Thanks, Doc!" and left.

"On the outside, Dr. Lumsden appeared confident; but on the inside, he was devastated. He knew that everything he had told this student was wrong.

"Dr. Lumsden had the integrity to face his new doubts honestly. He undertook a personal research project to check out the arguments for evolution, and over time, found them wanting. Based on the scientific evidence alone, he decided he must reject Darwinism, and he became a creationist. But as morning follows night, he had to face the next question, *Who is the Creator?* Shortly thereafter, by coincidence or not, his sister invited him to church. It was so out of character for this formerly crusty, self-confident evolutionist to go to church! Not much earlier, he would have had nothing to do with religion."

"But now, he was open to reconsider the identity of the Creator, and whether the claims of the Bible were true. His atheistic philosophy had also left him helpless to deal with guilt and bad habits in his personal life. This time he was open, and this time he heard the Good News that God had sent His Son to pay the penalty for our sins, and to offer men forgiveness and eternal life.

"A tremendous struggle was going on in Dr. Lumsden's heart as he listened to the sermon. When the service ended, the pastor gave an invitation to come to the front and decide once and for all, publicly, to receive Christ. Dr. Lumsden describes the turmoil he was in: 'With flesh protesting every inch of the way, I found myself walking forward, down to the altar. And there, found God! Truly, at that moment, I came to know Him, and received the Lord Jesus Christ as my Lord and Savior.' There's room at the cross even for know-it-all science professors, if they are willing to humble themselves and bow before the Creator to whom the scientific evidence points." [1]

Excuse Me Professor? I Have 40 Questions:

1. How and when did life begin?

2. How do we know that?

3. What existed before that?

4. If at one time nothing existed, how could anything exist now?

5. Where did the chemicals come from for life to begin?

6. What are the odds of them coming together by chance to form life from non-living matter?

   (F.Y.I. "Fred Hoyle and his colleague Chandra Wickramasinghe (*both world famous physicists*), calculated the odds that all the functional proteins necessary for life might originate by chance. They came up with a figure of one chance in 1040,000 (that's a 1 with 40,000 zeros after it)." Since Hoyle will not accept the Genesis account, he has adopted the theory that life must have come from other planets)![2]

7. Do you believe in the resurrection of the human body after death?

8. Why not?

9. What is spontaneous generation?

   (F.Y.I. Spontaneous generation is the idea that living cells sprang spontaneously from non-living matter.)

10. How is spontaneous generation significantly different from the idea of the resurrection of the dead?

11. Has spontaneous generation ever been observed in a laboratory?

12. What evidence is there to support the idea of spontaneous generation?

13. Since spontaneous generation has never been observed in a laboratory, how can it be called a scientific fact?

14. If scientists ever were successful in producing a living cell from non-living matter, wouldn't that only prove that intelligence was necessary to produce it?

15. Can you explain the differences between a hypothesis, a theory, and a scientific law?

   (F.Y.I. A hypothesis is an educated guess, based on observation, but has not been proven. A scientific theory summarizes a hypothesis when that hypothesis has been supported with repeated testing. A theory is valid as long as there is no evidence to dispute it. A law generalizes a body of observations. At the time it is made, no exceptions have been found to that law.)

16. Can you explain the difference between Micro-Evolution and Macro-Evolution?

17. What evidence is there that Macro-Evolution has occurred?

18. Why don't we see transitional forms walking around today?

19. Since Macro-Evolution has never been observed in a laboratory, how can it be taught as science?

20. What did Darwin say the fossil record would show if his theory was correct?

21. What does the fossil record show?

    (The answer is in Chapter 4, *Isn't Evolution a Proven Fact?*).

22. Why is evolution being taught as fact or even theory in light of the fact that the fossil record clearly points away from Darwin's ideas?

23. Some scientific laws or "laws of nature" include the law of gravity, the laws of motion, and the laws of thermodynamics.

24. Can you explain the second law of thermodynamics? Have the laws of thermodynamics ever been proven wrong?

25. How do you explain the clear contradiction between the laws of thermodynamics, which are among the most well established laws of science, and the theory of Macro-Evolution?

26. Astronomers tell us that there are 100 billion galaxies in the "known universe," and billions of stars in each galaxy. According to the laws of thermodynamics, if energy can neither be created nor destroyed, where did all the energy in the universe come from?

27. Is it true that Darwin said, in essence, that his theory of Macro-Evolution would stand or fall on what the fossil record would show?

28. How do you account for the fact that there are virtually no fossils showing any intermediate forms?

29. Isn't it true that the fossil record reveals fully formed kinds in their own right?

30. Why is it that the vast majority of us die between the ages of 40 and 80, no matter where we live or what we eat?

31. If evolution were true, why don't we see some people who live in relatively unpolluted areas living to be 200 to 300 years old?

32. What do we know about cells today that Darwin did not?

    (F.Y.I. Darwin believed that life could have originated by chance, in large part because he mistakenly believed that cells were very simple life forms).

33. So then, was Darwin correct in his assessment of the simplicity of cells?

34. Since Darwin was wrong about cells, which are the basic building blocks of life, how does that affect his theory of Macro-Evolution?

35. "Logic and mathematics are abstract principles that have been discovered rather than invented. We cannot do science, communicate, or navigate this world without them. They appear to stand outside of nature to describe and measure it. As Albert Einstein said, 'The most incomprehensible thing about the world is that it is comprehensible.' What is the source of math and logic?" [3]

36. Since so many young people are texting constantly, do you think we will begin to see babies being born with two thumbs on each hand anytime soon?

37. What are we to think of Nobel Prize winning scientists who say thing like, "Spontaneous generation is impossible but I believe it anyway?"

38. How much bias is there against the so-called "Intelligent Design" movement in universities and if so, why do you think that is?

39. If there is no such thing as right or wrong, how can you grade my papers?

40. If there is no such thing as right or wrong, or true and false, what is the point of going to college?

End Notes

1 David F. Coppedge, "*The World's Greatest Creation Scientists*" <www.creationsafaris.com/wgcs_5.htm>.

2 Fred Heeren, *Show Me God* (Wheeling. Searchlight Publications, 1995) p. 183.

3 From: *Questions for the Atheist* <www.Lifeway.com> Scott Pruett.

More on Jesus and His Words

To discover the truth about Jesus, you need to read His words yourself. Some of the world's most infamous people have been changed forever after reading the words of Jesus known as, "The Sermon on the Mount." It's found in Chapters 5-7 of Matthew.

Albert Einstein said: "As a child I received instruction both in the Bible and in the Talmud. I am a Jew, but I am enthralled by the luminous figure of the Nazarene. . . . No one can read the Gospels without feeling the actual presence of Jesus. His personality pulsates in every word. No myth is filled with such life." [1]

Truly, no man has ever spoken such words of love, wisdom, and compassion before or since. Here are just three chapters from the New Testament— Matthew 5-7. Can you find anyone who has ever spoken like this man?

The Words Of Christ

And when He saw the multitudes, He went up on the mountain; and after He sat down, His disciples came to Him.

And opening His mouth He {began} to teach them, saying,

"Blessed are the poor in spirit, for theirs is the kingdom of heaven.

"Blessed are those who mourn, for they shall be comforted.

"Blessed are the gentle, for they shall inherit the earth.

"Blessed are those who hunger and thirst for righteousness, for they shall be satisfied.

"Blessed are the merciful, for they shall receive mercy.

"Blessed are the pure in heart, for they shall see God.

"Blessed are the peacemakers, for they shall be called sons of God.

"Blessed are those who have been persecuted for the sake of righteousness, for theirs is the kingdom of heaven.

"Blessed are you when {men} cast insults at you, and persecute you, and say all kinds of evil against you falsely, on account of Me.

"Rejoice, and be glad, for your reward in heaven is great, for so they persecuted the prophets who were before you.

"You are the salt of the earth; but if the salt has become tasteless, how will it be made salty {again} It is good for nothing anymore, except to be thrown out and trampled under foot by men. [2]

"You are the light of the world. A city set on a hill cannot be hidden.

"Nor do {men} light a lamp, and put it under the peck-measure, but on the lampstand; and it gives light to all who are in the house.

"Let your light shine before men in such a way that they may see your good works, and glorify your Father who is in heaven.

"Do not think that I came to abolish the Law or the Prophets; I did not come to abolish, but to fulfill.

"For truly I say to you, until heaven and earth pass away, not the smallest letter or stroke shall pass away from the Law, until all is accomplished.

"Whoever then annuls one of the least of these commandments, and so teaches others, shall be called least in the kingdom of heaven; but whoever keeps and teaches {them,} he shall be called great in the kingdom of heaven.

"For I say to you, that unless your righteousness surpasses {that} of the scribes and Pharisees, you shall not enter the kingdom of heaven.

"You have heard that the ancients were told, 'You shall not commit murder' and 'Whoever commits murder shall be liable to the court.'

"But I say to you that everyone who is angry with his brother shall be guilty before the court; and whoever shall say to his brother, 'Raca,' shall be guilty before the supreme court; and whoever shall say, 'You fool,' shall be guilty {enough to go} into the fiery hell.

"If therefore you are presenting your offering at the altar, and there remember that your brother has something against you, leave your offering there before the altar, and go your way; first be reconciled to your brother, and then come and present your offering.

"Make friends quickly with your opponent at law while you are with him on the way, in order that your opponent may not deliver you to the judge, and the judge to the officer, and you be thrown into prison.

"Truly I say to you, you shall not come out of there, until you have paid up the last cent.

"You have heard that it was said, 'You shall not commit adultery'; but I say to you, that everyone who looks on a woman to lust for her has committed adultery with her already in his heart.

"And if your right eye makes you stumble, tear it out, and throw it from you; for it is better for you that one of the parts of your body perish, than for your whole body to be thrown into hell.

"And if your right hand makes you stumble, cut it off, and throw it from you; for it is better for you that one of the parts of your body perish, than for your whole body to go into hell.[3]

"And it was said, 'Whoever sends his wife away, let him give her a certificate of divorce'; but I say to you that everyone who divorces his wife, except for {the} cause of unchastity, makes her commit adultery; and whoever marries a divorced woman commits adultery.

"Again, you have heard that the ancients were told, 'You shall not make false vows, but shall fulfill your vows to the Lord.'

"But I say to you, make no oath at all, either by heaven, for it is the throne of God, or by the earth, for it is the footstool of His feet, or by Jerusalem, for it is the city of the great King.

"Nor shall you make an oath by your head, for you cannot make one hair white or black.

"But let your statement be, 'Yes, yes' {or} 'No, no'; and anything beyond these is of evil.

"You have heard that it was said, 'An eye for an eye, and a tooth for a tooth.'

"But I say to you, do not resist him who is evil; but whoever slaps you on your right cheek, turn to him the other also.

"And if anyone wants to sue you, and take your shirt, let him have your coat also.

"And whoever shall force you to go one mile, go with him two.

"Give to him who asks of you, and do not turn away from him who wants to borrow from you.

"You have heard that it was said, 'You shall love your neighbor, and hate your enemy.' "But I say to you, love your enemies, and pray for those who persecute you in order that you may be sons of your Father who is in heaven; for He causes His sun to rise on {the} evil and {the} good, and sends rain on {the} righteous and {the} unrighteous.

"For if you love those who love you, what reward have you? Do not even the tax-gatherers do the same?

"And if you greet your brothers only, what do you do more {than others} Do not even the Gentiles do the same?

"Therefore you are to be perfect, as your heavenly Father is perfect.

Chapter 6

"Beware of practicing your righteousness before men to be noticed by them; otherwise you have no reward with your Father who is in heaven.

"When therefore you give alms, do not sound a trumpet before you, as the hypocrites do in the synagogues and in the streets, that they may be honored by men. Truly I say to you, they have their reward in full.

"But when you give alms, do not let your left hand know what your right hand is doing that your alms may be "in secret; and your Father who sees in secret will repay you.

"And when you pray, you are not to be as the hypocrites; for they love to stand and pray in the synagogues and on the street corners, in order to be seen by men. Truly I say to you, they have their reward in full.

"But you, when you pray, go into your inner room, and when you have shut your door, pray to your Father who is in secret, and your Father who sees in secret will repay you.

"And when you are praying, do not use meaningless repetition, as the Gentiles do, for they suppose that they will be heard for their many words.

"Therefore do not be like them; for your Father knows what you need, before you ask Him.

"Pray, then, in this way: 'Our Father who art in heaven, Hallowed be Thy name.

'Thy kingdom come. Thy will be done, On earth as it is in heaven.

'Give us this day our daily bread.

'And forgive us our debts, as we also have forgiven our debtors.

'And do not lead us into temptation, but deliver us from evil. [For Thine is the kingdom, and the power, and the glory, forever. Amen.]'

"For if you forgive men for their transgressions, your heavenly Father will also forgive you.

"But if you do not forgive men, then your Father will not forgive your transgressions.

"And whenever you fast, do not put on a gloomy face as the hypocrites {do,} for they neglect their appearance in order to be seen fasting by men. Truly I say to you, they have their reward in full.

"But you, when you fast, anoint your head, and wash your face so that you may not be seen fasting by men, but by your Father who is in secret; and your Father who sees in secret will repay you.

"Do not lay up for yourselves treasures upon earth, where moth and rust destroy, and where thieves break in and steal.

"But lay up for yourselves treasures in heaven, where neither moth nor rust destroys, and where thieves do not break in or steal; for where your treasure is, there will your heart be also.

"The lamp of the body is the eye; if therefore your eye is clear, your whole body will be full of light.

"But if your eye is bad, your whole body will be full of darkness. If therefore the light that is in you is darkness, how great is the darkness! [4]

"No one can serve two masters; for either he will hate the one and love the other, or he will hold to one and despise the other. You cannot serve God and mammon (material wealth).

"For this reason I say to you, do not be anxious for your life, {as to} what you shall eat, or what you shall drink; nor for your body, {as to} what you shall put on. Is not life more than food, and the body than clothing?

"Look at the birds of the air, that they do not sow, neither do they reap, nor gather into barns, and {yet} your heavenly Father feeds them. Are you not worth much more than they?

"And which of you by being anxious can add a {single} cubit to his life's span?

"And why are you anxious about clothing? Observe how the lilies of the field grow; they do not toil nor do they spin, yet I say to you that even Solomon in all his glory did not clothe himself like one of these.

"But if God so arrays the grass of the field, which is {alive} today and tomorrow is thrown into the furnace, {will He} not much more {do so for} you, O men of little faith?

"Do not be anxious then, saying, 'What shall we eat?' or 'What shall we drink?' or 'With what shall we clothe ourselves?'

"For all these things the Gentiles eagerly seek; for your heavenly Father knows that you need all these things.

"But seek first His kingdom and His righteousness; and all these things shall be added to you.

"Therefore do not be anxious for tomorrow; for tomorrow will care for itself. {Each} day has enough trouble

Chapter 7

"Do not judge lest you be judged.

"For in the way you judge, you will be judged; and by your standard of measure, it will be measured to you.

"And why do you look at the speck that is in your brother's eye, but do not notice the log that is in your own eye?

"Or how can you say to your brother, 'Let me take the speck out of your eye,' and behold, the log is in your own eye?

"You hypocrite, first take the log out of your own eye, and then you will see clearly to take the speck out of your brother's eye.

"Do not give what is holy to dogs, and do not throw your pearls before swine, lest they trample them under their feet, and turn and tear you to pieces.

"Ask, and it shall be given to you; seek, and you shall find; knock, and it shall be opened to you.

"For everyone who asks receives, and he who seeks finds, and to him who knocks it shall be opened.

"Or what man is there among you, when his son shall ask him for a loaf, will give him a stone?

"Or if he shall ask for a fish, he will not give him a snake, will he?

"If you then, being evil, know how to give good gifts to your children, how much more shall your Father who is in heaven give what is good to those who ask Him!

"Therefore, however you want people to treat you, so treat them, for this is the Law and the Prophets.

"Enter by the narrow gate; for the gate is wide, and the way is broad that leads to destruction, and many are those who enter by it.

"For the gate is small, and the way is narrow that leads to life, and few are those who find it.

"Beware of the false prophets, who come to you in sheep's clothing, but inwardly are ravenous wolves.

"You will know them by their fruits. Grapes are not gathered from thorn {bushes,} nor figs from thistles, are they?

"Even so, every good tree bears good fruit; but the bad tree bears bad fruit.

"A good tree cannot produce bad fruit, nor can a bad tree produce good fruit.

"Every tree that does not bear good fruit is cut down and thrown into the fire.

"So then, you will know them by their fruits.

"Not everyone who says to Me, 'Lord, Lord,' will enter the kingdom of heaven; but he who does the will of My Father who is in heaven.

"Many will say to Me on that day, 'Lord, Lord, did we not prophesy in Your name, and in Your name cast out demons, and in Your name perform many miracles?'

"And then I will declare to them, 'I never knew you; depart from Me, you who practice lawlessness.'

"Therefore everyone who hears these words of Mine, and acts upon them, may be compared to a wise man, who built his house upon the rock.

"And the rain descended, and the floods came, and the winds blew, and burst against that house; and {yet} it did not fall, for it had been founded upon the rock.

"And everyone who hears these words of Mine, and does not act upon them, will be like a foolish man, who built his house upon the sand.

"And the rain descended, and the floods came, and the winds blew, and burst against that house; and it fell, and great was its fall."

The result was that when Jesus had finished these words, the multitudes were amazed at His teaching; for He was teaching them as {one} having authority, and not as their scribes."

The following quotes and essays reveal the uniqueness of Jesus.

The Life Of Christ, By Philip Schaff

"This Jesus of Nazareth, without money and arms, conquered more millions than Alexander, Caesar, Mohammed, and Napoleon; without science and learning, He shed more light on things human and divine than all philosophers and scholars combined; without the eloquence of schools, He spoke such words of life as were never spoken before or since and produced effects which lie beyond the reach of orator or poet; without writing a single line, He set more pens in motion, and furnished themes for more sermons, orations, discussions, learned volumes, works of art, and songs of praise, than the whole army of great men of ancient and modern times."

The Famous Essay, *One Solitary Life*

"Here is a man who was born in an obscure village, the child of a peasant woman. He grew up in another village. He worked in a carpenter shop until He was thirty, and then for three years He was an itinerant preacher. He never owned a home. He never wrote a book. He never held an office. He never had a family. He never went to college. He never put his foot inside a big city. He never traveled two hundred miles from the place where He was born. He never did one of the things that usually accompany greatness. He had no credentials but Himself. While still a young man, the tide of popular opinion turned against Him. His friends ran away. One of them denied Him. He was turned over to His enemies. He went through the mockery of a trial. He was nailed upon a cross between two thieves. While He was dying His executers gambled for the only piece of property He had on earth—His coat. When He was dead, He was taken down and laid in a borrowed grave through the pity of a friend.

"Nineteen long centuries have come and gone, and today He is the centerpiece of the human race and the leader of the column of progress. I am far within the mark when I say that all the armies that ever marched, all the navies that ever were built, all the parliaments that ever sat and all the kings that ever reigned, put together, have not affected the life of man on this earth as powerfully as has that one solitary life."

The Incomparable Christ

"More than nineteen hundred years ago there was a Man born contrary to the laws of life. This Man lived in poverty and was reared in obscurity. He did not travel extensively. Only once did He cross the boundary of the country in which He lived; that was during His exile in childhood.

"He possessed neither wealth nor influence. His relatives were inconspicuous and had neither training nor formal education. In infancy He startled a king; in childhood He puzzled doctors; in manhood He ruled the course of nature, walked upon the billows as if pavements, and hushed the sea to sleep. He healed the multitudes without medicine and made no charge for His service.

"He never wrote a book, and yet all the libraries of the country could not hold the books that have been written about Him. He never wrote a song, and yet He has furnished the theme for more songs than all the song writers combined.

"He never founded a college, but all the schools put together cannot boast of having as many students. He never marshaled an army, nor drafted a soldier, nor fired a gun; and yet no leader ever had more volunteers who have, under His orders, made more rebels stack arms and surrender without a shot fired.

"He never practiced psychiatry, and yet He healed more broken hearts than all the doctors far and near. Once each week the wheels of commerce cease their turning and multitudes wend their way to worshipping assemblies to pay homage and respect to Him.

"The names of the past proud statesmen of Greece and Rome have come and gone. The names of the past scientists, philosophers, and theologians have come and gone; but the name of this Man abounds more and more. Though time has spread nineteen hundred years between the people of this generation and the scene of His crucifixion, yet He still lives. Herod could not destroy Him, and the grave could not hold Him.

"He stands forth upon the highest pinnacle of heavenly glory, proclaimed of God, acknowledged by angels, adored by saints, and feared by devils, as the living, personal Christ, our Lord and Savior."

Napoleon Bonaparte

"Christ alone has succeeded in so raising the mind of man towards the unseen that it becomes insensible to the barriers of time and space. Across the chasm of eighteen hundred years Jesus Christ makes a demand which is beyond all others difficult to satisfy. He asks for that which a philosopher may often seek in vain at the hands of his friends, or a father of his children, or a bride of her spouse, or a man of his brother. He asks for the human heart; He will have it entirely to Himself; He demands it unconditionally, and forthwith His demand is granted. Its powers and faculties become an annexation to the empire of Christ. All who sincerely believe in Him experience that supernatural love towards Him. This phenomenon is unaccountable; it is altogether beyond the scope of man's creative powers. Time, the great destroyer can neither exhaust its strength nor put a limit to its range."

A Final Thought

"As for the days of our life, they contain seventy years, or if due to strength, eighty years, yet their pride is {but} labor and sorrow; for soon it is gone and we fly away.

"Who understands the power of Thine anger, and Thy fury, according to the fear that is due Thee?

"So teach us to number our days, that we may present to Thee a heart of wisdom."

— Psalm 90:10-12.

End Notes

1. Einstein in an interview with George Sylvester Viereck, "What Life Means to Einstein", The Saturday Evening Post, October 26, 1929, Curtis Publishing Company.

2. In verse 13 of Matthew chapter 5, salt is a stable compound, it does not "lose its flavor." The problem is in the English translation of the original Greek, it should have been translated, "If the salt is not used for the purpose it was designed for, it is good for nothing."

3. In Matthew 5:29-30, Jesus is speaking figuratively since cutting off your hand or plucking out your eye would not stop a person from sinning, that is a matter of the heart. While it is literally true that it would be better to go to heaven with only one hand or one eye than hell with two, Jesus is saying that we should develop an eternal perspective, see sin for what it is and cut it off at the source whatever that may be.

4. In Matthew 6:22-23, the phrase "good eye" and "bad eye" was a Hebrew idiom; if you had a "bad eye" it meant you were a stingy person, and if you had a "good eye" you were a generous person.

5. I am indebted to Josh McDowell's *Evidence that Demands a Verdict* for the essays used in this chapter.